ACADEMIC SPOKEN ENGLISH
A CORPUS-BASED GUIDE TO LECTURES, PRESENTATIONS, SEMINARS AND TUTORIALS

Academic Spoken English

A Corpus-Based Guide to Lectures, Presentations, Seminars and Tutorials

Kristin Blanpain and An Laffut

Acco Leuven / Den Haag

First edition: 2009
Second edition: 2012

Published by
Uitgeverij Acco, Blijde Inkomststraat 22, 3000 Leuven, België
E-mail: uitgeverij@acco.be – Website: www.uitgeverijacco.be

For the Netherlands:
Acco Nederland, Westvlietweg 67 F, 2495 AA Den Haag, Nederland
E-mail: info@uitgeverijacco.nl – Website: www.uitgeverijacco.nl

Cover design: www.frisco-ontwerpbureau.be

© 2009 by Acco (Academische Coöperatieve Vennootschap cvba), Leuven (België)
No part of this book may be reproduced in any form, by mimeograph, film or any other means without permission in writing from the publisher.

D/2009/0543/285   NUR 632   ISBN 978-90-334-7626-6

Table of Contents

PREFACE	7

Part One	**PRESENTING AND LECTURING**	9
Unit I	**Features of spoken language**	11
1. Spoken and written language		11
2. Colloquial vocabulary		15
Unit II	**Structure**	17
1. Outlining		17
2. Signposting		19
3. Highlighting and clarifying		25
Unit III	**Referring to visuals**	29
1. The language of graphics		29
2. Using numerals		33
Unit IV	**Delivery**	35
1. Speaking to your audience		35
2. Chunking and emphasis		36
3. Guidelines for visuals		39
4. Practice makes perfect		40
Part Two	**INTERACTING WITH COLLEAGUES AND STUDENTS**	41
Unit I	**Handling the question-and-answer session**	43
1. Asking questions		43
2. Responding to questions and objections		49

Unit II	**Chairing a conference session**	53
1. Guidelines for chairing		53
2. Introducing a plenary speaker		55
3. Thanking a speaker		59
Unit III	**Tutoring students**	61
1. Giving instructions		61
2. Making suggestions		62
3. Giving feedback: encouragement and criticism		65
Unit IV	**Dealing with practicalities**	69
1. Classroom language		69
2. Infrastructure and equipment		71

Part Three	**IMPROVING SPOKEN LANGUAGE**	75
Unit I	**Expanding vocabulary**	77
Unit II	**Avoiding common errors**	83
1. Vocabulary		83
2. Grammar		85
Adjectives and adverbs		85
Articles		86
Conditionals		87
Countable and uncountable nouns		88
Pronouns		89
Verb forms and tenses		91
Dutchisms		92
Unit III	**Improving pronunciation**	93
1. Word stress		93
2. Consonants		98
3. Vowels		101

KEY TO THE EXERCISES   105

Preface

In an internationalised academic environment, lecturers and researchers increasingly need to use English to give lectures and presentations, to participate in seminars and conferences and to coach international students.

This book offers help in a wide range of areas, from expanding spoken academic vocabulary to improving delivery. It is informed by actual presentation and teaching practice: examples and exercises are based on the MICASE Corpus and the John Swales Conference Corpus, extensive collections of transcripts of lectures and presentations, ensuring relevance and authenticity.

The material is presented in short chapters, organized into three parts.

PART ONE – PRESENTING AND LECTURING

The first part deals with typical "presentation skills," from using appropriate language to effective delivery. Particular attention is devoted to the use of so-called "signposts": phrases such as *moving on to the second point* or *to go back to what we were discussing earlier* are useful because they provide structure, but non-native speakers' range of signposts is often very limited. For this reason, many examples of typical "presentation phrases" are provided. Part One also contains a separate chapter on referring to visuals, such as graphs and charts.

PART TWO – INTERACTING WITH COLLEAGUES AND STUDENTS

In a presentation and lecturing context, the greatest challenge is posed by moments of unscripted interaction, where you need to "think on your feet": the question-and-answer session at the end of a presentation or lecture, for instance, is challenging for both the speaker and the participants. The same is true for interaction with students during lectures or tutorials. In such situations, it is again highly useful to have a wide range of typical phrases at your disposal that you can use almost automatically. This part also includes a chapter on practical and logistical aspects, such as referring to equipment or the lay-out of a building.

PART THREE – IMPROVING SPOKEN LANGUAGE

The final part focuses on spoken language skills. Unit I provides additional vocabulary practice, focusing mainly on colloquial vocabulary. Unit II contains an overview of common errors, mainly (but not exclusively) those made by speakers of Dutch. Where necessary, short, practical grammar rules are provided. Unit III deals with pronunciation problems and is accompanied by audio files that can be downloaded from the Acco website (www.uitgeverijacco.be/academicspokenenglish) with the code you find on page 93.

Throughout the book, considerable attention is paid to typical presentation and interaction vocabulary. Two comments should be made in this respect:
- Many chapters contain a large number of typical phrases The best approach is to focus on two or three new expressions at a time and to consciously use these in a presentation or lecturing context. In this way, you can gradually expand your "repertoire".
- The key to successful language learning is to focus on "collocations" (i.e. word partnerships such as *make a point* or *in due course*). In examples and exercises, such collocations have therefore been highlighted in bold

The book can be used in the context of a presentation skills course or as a self-study resource. A key to all exercises is included.

ACKNOWLEDGMENTS

We wish to express our gratitude to the following people for their help in producing this book. Colette Coppens, Ian Morrison and Jane Morrison, for recording the sound files accompanying the pronunciation exercises, and Lut Sengier, for technical assistance. Ute Römer, for kindly granting us permission to use excerpts and examples from MICASE and the John Swales Conference Corpus. John Harbord, for generously allowing us to insert an email on presentation style. And Serge Verlinde, for his support and advice.

PART ONE

Presenting and Lecturing

UNIT I
Features of spoken language

1. Spoken and written language

Unlike readers of a text, listeners do not have the opportunity to backtrack, pause, or process the message at their own pace. To facilitate comprehension, the language of your presentation should therefore be different from the language used in an article.

1.1   **Skim these 3 excerpts from lectures and note down any differences with written prose.**

- EXCERPT 1

    Anybody need copies of handouts...? Any questions from last time? Any comments? Well if not I'd like to start now with the derivation of the cycle time for unit load automated storage retrieval systems. Some of the material, not all of it, comes from a paper that uh White and John White and I published in 1984 so it's been a while, uh this is not all of the material mind you okay so there's some extensions that you're gonna see in class, which are not shown in the paper, but some of the basic derivations are here, this is the... <writing on board> Bozer and White paper... IIE transactions, I won't write the title but it's called Travel Time Models for Automated Storage Retrieval Systems... volume... well I may not have the volume number here... yeah I just ... yeah volume sixteen number four... and as I said it's a fairly old paper nineteen ... eighty-four.
    Mkay so if you want a copy of the paper you can, go read it uh, it's not it's not required that you get this paper though... okay, last time... we defined what we mean we ... what we mean by a single-command cycle dual-command cycle so I hope you remember those. And, for today's lecture, we're gonna assume the IO point is at the lower left-hand corner of the rack. This week and next you're gonna see some extensions where we look at alternative I-O point locations in the rack. So to start our derivation let's look at uh our assumptions first... a couple of these assumptions are pretty restrictive... but we're gonna see how to relax them in no particular sequence here here are the assumptions. (MICASE)

- EXCERPT 2

    And that's a problem with human research. Um, but ... there was a a whole series of of experiments, most of them in cats by a guy named Barry Jacobs at Princeton at this time so this is getting into the seventies, early eighties now. Where ... basically what he did was characterize the behavioral profile of a whole variety of hallucinogen- hallucinogenic agents in cats as as well as a bunch of studies in rats. Okay so he he just looked at the behavior of the animals very carefully when they were given mescaline or LSD or uh, uh psilocybin and a whole variety of hallucinogens. And, what he found was is that animals show very characteristic changes in their patterns of behavior, under hallucinogens, that are unique, that is they're different than the patterns of behaviors you see under psychostimulants or under opiates, under amphetamine under cocaine under PCP. (MICASE)

- EXCERPT 3

    Um, let's talk about psychological tests. So there's interviewing, um, which is my personal favorite way of trying to figure out what's going on. But there're also tests, and these can be used obviously in a much broader sense you can give the test to a lot of people at the same time ... um sometimes they can be very helpful in trying to get a grip on ... um specific issues that you're trying to assess

    And when we talk about tests we always have to talk about validity and reliability, and this is stuff that is probably familiar to you from Introductory Psychology. Uh, all these kinds of validity that you have here on your, um, in your notes, are fancy names for what is basically common sense. And since you've got the definitions right there i'm gonna go through this pretty fast, and just give you examples. Face validity is that you're giving a test that measures what it appears to measure. Um, basically if you're asking, if you're doing a test of anxiety you want your questions to look like they're anxiety questions. You want them to ha- say things like you know do you ever feel panicked or nervous, does your stomach ever feel upset, do you ever have a hard time falling asleep right very sort of straightforward ... tests should be look like tests of what they are. (MICASE)

Typical features of spoken language

- VOCABULARY
    - use of colloquial words and phrases (e.g. *stuff, lots of, pretty fast*)
    - use of approximation and vague language (e.g. *these kinds of ..., sort of ...*)

- SYNTAX
    - less complex sentences
    - coordination (e.g. *and, so, but*) rather than subordination (e.g. *although, resulting in*)

- DISCOURSE STRUCTURE
  - typical discourse markers: *Now, OK, So, Well, Right*
  - repetition and redundancy
  - previewing and reviewing (e.g. *What this boils down to is ...*)
  - references to "here and now" (e.g. *As I said earlier, As you can see from the graph ...*)

The audience will find it difficult to follow your talk
- if lexical density is too high (= the proportion of content words to the total discourse)
  After reviewing the nature and the extent of the recent growth of business services in Britain, the wider significance of such growth will be examined.
  I will first review the nature of the recent growth of business services in Britain and try to determine how large this growth is. Then, I will go on to examine the wider significance of such an increase.

- if you frequently use nominalisation
  Discussion of these factors will be followed by the **identification** of a number of conclusions common to both countries.
  → I will first **discuss** these factors, and then **identify** a number of conclusions that are common to both countries.

- if the verb is too far removed from the subject;
  Our attempt to confirm the association between asymptomatic bacteriuria and increased mortality among ambulatory elderly women **failed**.
  → **We were unable** to confirm the association between asymptomatic bacteriuria and increased mortality among ambulatory elderly women.

1.2 Rewrite the following sentences to make them more suitable for a spoken register.

1. The present research project comprises methods development and application of mathematical simulations to real world engineering problems in three principal areas.

2. Far right ideologies have therefore been the focus of renewed academic and – since the recent European election – political interest.

3. New research into the effects of sedentary behaviour has called into question the commonly held assumption that obesity and TV viewing are directly related.

4. In this section, some of the basic tenets of Young's argument are examined and compared with existing textbook interpretations. The latter are shown to be extremely reductive, as they ignore both Young's interest in non-empirical conditions and his criticism of the traditional understanding of the transcendental.

5. Improving quality of information for patients is a question of the media used, but equally of the quality of the content, currently a much neglected area.

6. Despite its high prevalence in this patient population, depression remains one of the most underdiagnosed and thus undertreated disorders, exerting detrimental effects on cellular immunity, including those aspects of the immune system affected by HIV.

7. Thus, the assumption of a causal relationship between employee satisfaction and increased productivity made in the study can be questioned on the basis that it might lead to overestimates as well as to underestimates of the competitiveness effect.

Features of spoken language

2. Colloquial vocabulary

> "Academic style is not used in all academic settings. Lectures are generally delivered in a relatively non-academic style. It is not uncommon to hear lecturers use words and phrases like stuff, things, bunch or a whole lot of which would not be appropriate for an academic writing task"[1]

2.1 **The following pages contain examples of colloquial phrases in spoken contexts. Select 3 that you would like to use yourself in the course of a presentation or lecture.**

Getting started

I'll first give you the framework, and then I'll **flesh it out**
Could we just **pick up where we left off** yesterday?
OK, so **we're all done with** methods, and today we're **going on to** biopsychology.
Let's begin with **just a quick recap** of last week.
I want **to start off** today by saying a few things about...
And there are a few others that I'll just **run through** really quickly.

Coming up against problems

There are many ways of **tackling** this kind of problem.
And now we're getting into some **tricky** territory.
There were hardly any data to fall back on, so we had to **start from scratch.**
The procedure seems **pretty straightforward** but ...
It is difficult **to pin down** the factors involved.
This kind of problem has **cropped up** before.
As you can see, it **does a pretty bad job** of estimating temperatures in South America.
We're still struggling to **figure out how we might be able to integrate this in the research.**

Recapitulating & winding down

Let me first **recap**.
Let me just **backtrack** a little.
What this **boils down to** is this.
I think that **pretty much covers** everything we need.

---

1. JOHN M. SWALES & CHRISTINE B. FEAK (1994), *Academic Writing for Graduate Students*, Ann Arbor: University of Michigan Press, p. 15.

2.2 **Insert the correct prepositions.**

1. Are you .... **me**?
2. Could we just **pick** .... where we **left** .... yesterday?
3. I'll try to help with the problems you **come** .... **with**.
4. That **goes** .... **saying**.
5. I'll talk about that .... **due course**.
6. Let's **leave** it .... that.
7. This is a point we'll **pick** .... later on.
8. I probably **touched** .... this subject briefly.
9. I think that really **wraps** .... that part.

2.3 **One of the best ways to make your spoken English more natural is to use some of the many expressions with the verb *get*. Complete the sentences below with an appropriate word from the box.**

HANG – ON – TO – DOWN – GOING

1. So, let's just **get** .... **with it**.
2. He's the one who **got** all this ....
3. I'm going to start with our general rationale and then I'll **get** .... **to** some details.
4. This raises another interesting issue, but I'll **get** .... that in a minute.
5. Don't worry. You'll soon **get the** .... **of it**.

INTO – ACROSS – DOWN – BACK – STARTED

1. Perhaps **we'd better get** ....
2. Okay, well now we'll **get** .... **to** the hard part.
3. That information's back at the office so I'll have to **get** .... **to** you later.
4. The message I really want to **get** .... is that we shouldn't be too quick to dismiss the impact on the economy.
5. I'll **get** .... this a bit more specifically as I move on.

Part III, Unit 1 contains additional practice on colloquial vocabulary.

UNIT II

Structure

1. Outlining

Many speeches and presentations start in the following manner.

> GETTING STARTED
> Good morning. I would like to thank the organisers for the opportunity of speaking here today …
>
> SETTING THE SCENE
> There has been much interest in the past few years in the issues of ….. Whilst there are still many unsolved problems here, our focus has shifted somewhat towards ….
>
> STATING YOUR PURPOSE
> In this presentation, I will show how some of the methods we have used previously for ….. can be applied in this context and how we have tackled some of the other questions ….
>
> OUTLINING STRUCTURE OF THE TALK
> First, I will outline the objectives – what is the need we are addressing?
> In a second part I will discuss one way we have found useful for …
> Thirdly I will illustrate how we have addressed some aspects of …
> And finally, I will summarise the main points and draw some conclusions on …

Similarly, lecturers usually start by briefly announcing what will be covered in the lecture and often include a short recap of the previous class.

> **Good morning. Today we're going to be talking about** polyprotic acids, which are acids that have more than one easily ionizable hydrogen, and among the most important of these are the amino acids, which exist in proteins and peptides, **and**

> so we're going move to those as soon as we _ cover some of the basics, with _ some simpler, polyprotic acids. I have on the board acetic acid, as the _ archetypal carboxylic acid, and then i have two... diprotic acids, succinic acid <pause while writing on blackboard> and adipic acid. (MICASE)

> The topic for today's lecture is river floodplains, and **what we're gonna be doing is, first I wanna talk about** the larger picture what it means, a watershed is and what drainage basins are. **And then we'll look at** some specific drainage patterns which are actually, on page ninety-five I think, yeah in your coursepack. **And then we'll talk about** the different processes, that are, that go on surrounding a river, **followed by** the specific landforms of the floodplain, the climate of the floodplain, soils and vegetation of the floodplain. **And then if we have time we'll look at** slides, of, um last week's lab, when we went to Sharon Hollow. **Okay, so the first thing, is** talking about this idea of a ... (MICASE)

> Uh let me ask a positive question how many folks know how to, on a Mac know how to read Windows software...? Okay. Not, not enough. Okay so we we'll figure something out... Okay there's one more issue with the readings but I think I can get to that more naturally as part of the _ the discussion **so let's get started**. <pause> **Let's begin with** _ just **a quick recap of** _ **last week,** in which we collapsed _ something like three or four centuries of development into _ basically two two class meetings and so didn't do it nearly as much justice as, as it deserves. But **here's what we saw. Sort of the main points**... that the Enlightenment and machine production of factories_ basically dealt a mortal blow to to feudal- to the system of feudalism in in Europe. (MICASE)

It is important that this part is not dealt with too quickly. The audience needs time to adjust, so don't rush through your first slides or your introductory remarks.

1.1 Below you will find a number of ways of stating the purpose of your presentation. In pairs, complete the sentences using the words given. Take turns: student A combines the 3 sentences with the number 1. Then B does the same with those numbered 2 etc. Repeat the exercise, until you can use these phrases automatically.[2]

---

2. Format based on MARK POWELL (1996), *Presenting in English*.

19 ▶ Structure

In this presentation/lecture, I'd like to

TALK   INTRODUCE   EXPLORE   TAKE   REPORT   TELL

1. .... **to you about** our project.
2. .... **you about** my research.
3. .... **you to** the fascinating topic of data protection.
4. .... **a look at** the impact of the media on our everyday lives.
5. .... **on** the results of a study on risk analysis.
6. .... the issue of school effectiveness.

I'll start by

MAKING   DESCRIBING   BRINGING   GIVING   FILLING   LOOKING

1. .... **you in on** the general background.
2. .... a few preliminary **remarks** on the methodology I used.
3. .... **you up-to-date on** developments at EU level.
4. .... recent technological developments.
5. .... **you an overview** of current theories.
6. .... **at** the main indicators of school effectiveness.

... and then I'll go on to

PUT   DISCUSS   MAKE   HIGHLIGHT   TAKE

1. .... **you through** a couple of practical applications.
2. .... **the implications** of my results.
3. .... a number of **recommendations** to improve existing legislation.
4. .... the situation **into** some kind of **perspective**.
5. .... three key methodological features.
6. .... **how** internal school processes influence learning.

2. Signposting

The overall structure should not only be referred to at the start of a presentation or lecture. It is important to remind listeners of the structure and to indicate transitions. This is done by the use of discourse markers, also called "signposts". A typical problem for many non-native speakers, even if they are fairly fluent in English, is that they lack this type of vocabulary. As a result, the different parts of their talk are not well "glued together".

2.1 Study the following signposting expressions for a few minutes. What is the underlying metaphor? Cover the page and try to recall 10 different expressions.

*I should state **at the outset** that the goal here is not **to arrive** at truly predictive models.*
*A lot of this lecture will be concerned with **going over ground we've covered before**.*
*Let me just **go over** that argument very quickly. I hope you don't **get lost** in the details.*
*Feel free to ask any questions you like **as we go along**.*

***Moving on** to the question of the US market, ...*
*That **brings us to** the second point ...*
*But before we get into that, can I just **jump ahead** to ...*
*We'll take a **shortcut** here.*
*We'll **come back to** the different types of data.*

***To go back** for a moment to what we were discussing earlier, ...*
***To return to** our analogy, how do we avoid the ...*
*Let me just **backtrack a little**.*
*What I've done is **skipped** the second step.*

***To digress** for a moment, let's consider ...*
*But let's not get **sidetracked**.*
*I'm **getting a little ahead** of myself.*
***To get back to** what I was saying.*

2.2 Test your signposting language.

What would you say if you wanted	Now find an alternative on the following pages
To mark the transition to a new topic	
To direct your audience's attention to a graph or slide	
To paraphrase	
To introduce an example	
To refer to a previous point	

Structure

What would you say if you wanted	Now find an alternative on the following pages
TO SUMMARIZE SOME POINTS YOU HAVE MADE	
TO CONCLUDE	
TO INVITE QUESTIONS	

The following pages offer a range of signposts commonly used in presentations and lectures. A useful approach is to select two or three phrases that you plan to use during your next talk. Once these have become part of your repertoire, you can select a few new phrases for active use. In this way, you can gradually expand your range of phrases.

Getting started

Now, what I'd like to do today is ...
The focus of my presentation is on ...
I'm going to divide my presentation into four parts ...
X consists of / comprises three categories. First, ... A second category ...
In particular, my focus is on ...
So, what are we going to cover today?

Referring to a previous point

As for methodology, I already mentioned that ...
Let's go back to ... for a moment ...
Going back to a point I made earlier ...
As I said at the outset ...

Starting or announcing a new point

The next point is ...
OK, now ... (falling intonation + pause)
Right ... (falling intonation + pause)
Well, let's turn to the question, what can we do?
That brings us to ...
Moving on to ... / To move on to ... / If I could just move on to ...

This principle also extends to ... as I will mention in a moment.
I'll talk about that in due course.
I'm gonna come back to these in a second, but for now...
And finally we have ...
Any other comments before I turn to ...?

Referring to visuals (see also Unit III)

I'd like you to look at this chart ...
The graph we're looking at very clearly demonstrates that ...
I'd like to draw your attention to ...
The vertical / horizontal axis represents ...
If you look at the third sentence, you'll notice that ...
Let's take a closer look for a moment at ...

Giving an example / elaborating

I'll just mention one example.
To give you an example.
Take X ...
One of the most common ... is ...
I'd like to expand on that a little before we move on ...
To elaborate on that a little for those of you who aren't familiar with ...

Expressing reasons & connections

There's a pretty obvious reason why.
So this means that ...
On top of that ...
And, what's more, it's also ...
This ties in with ...

Restating

All this says is ...
My point is that ...
To put that another way, ...
Basically, it comes down to this ....
So, in other words, what I'm saying is that ...
This is not to say that ....

Aside markers

Incidentally, you might again want to compare this with ...
By the way, ...

X doesn't really concern us here at the moment ...
To digress for a moment, let's consider ...
Let me just make a parenthesis.
Perhaps I should just mention that ...

Inviting questions

Right?
Do you see what I'm saying?
Does that make sense?
Any questions on this part? No? So, shall we talk about part B then?
Before we get going with the next unit, are there any questions about anything?

Summarizing

In conclusion ...
I'd like to conclude, if I may, by ...
In short, ...
To tie this up ...
OK so (level intonation, no pause) what I've done is to ...
OK, I think I'll leave it there.
OK, I think that I've covered everything I wanted to.
Well, that more or less wraps things up.
To recap on the main points ...
What I have been arguing in this lecture is ...
So the key point to bear in mind is ...
Any questions before we wrap up? Okay, that concludes it then, thanks.

Do not finish a presentation abruptly. Wind down gently with a carefully prepared conclusion, thank the audience and invite questions.

I hope I have shed some light on ... I would now be happy to take your questions.
I would now be happy to answer any questions you may have.
If you have any questions, I'd be pleased to answer them now.
So with that I'll quit. Thank you very much.
So I'll stop there and I hope we can have some questions. Thank you.

2.3 Which of these discourse markers are typical of conversational style?

In addition – anyhow – furthermore – therefore – by the way – let me recap – what's more – incidentally – OK so – in conclusion – right – well – actually – the thing is – by contrast – and besides

2.4 Fill the gaps.

1. A lot of this lecture will be concerned with **g**............ **over ground** we've **co**................ before.
2. Feel free to ask .... **questions** you like as we go along.
3. I'll talk about that **in d**................ **course**.
4. I'll **touch** .... this subject very **br**................ .
5. Well, let's **t**................ **to** the question, what can we do?
6. That **b**................ **me to** my second point.
7. **M**................ **on to** methodology, I would like to highlight two things.
8. I'd like to .... **your attention to** the vertical axis.
9. Let's **take a closer** .... these figures.
10. **To p**................ **that another way**, we define meaning in terms of human assumptions.

2.5 Fill the gaps.

1. I'd like to **e**............... **on that** a little before we move on.
2. I'll just **m**............... **one example**.
3. So, basically, multilevel governance .... **down to** three things.
4. So, to **get b**............... **to** what I was saying, ...
5. .... **I said** at the outset, this is a highly complex process.
6. I should **j**............... **mention** one thing before I go on.
7. Sorry, perhaps I didn't **make myself** ....
8. So, **just to give you the main p**............... again, ...
9. Well, that more or less **w**............... **things up**.
10. I hope I have **s**............... **some light** on this issue.
11. So I think I'll **l**............... **it at that**. Thank you.
12. I would now be happy to **t**............... **your questions**.

3. **Highlighting and clarifying**

Good presentations not only have a clear macro-structure, but they are also well-structured at the micro-level. This involves some didactic skills: you need to be able focus your audience's attention on the main points and to explain difficult aspects adequately.

- HIGHLIGHTING

The following devices can be used to highlight important / new topics and points:

Topic markers

> With regard to ...
> The question then is ... / and then perhaps the most important question is ...
> Now, turning to ...
> Let's move on to ...
> On to ...

Pseudo-cleft constructions (*What .... is ....*)

> What accountants do is spread it over several years
> What I want to do is simply reorganize all that information.
> What I've done is skip the second step.
> So, what we're aiming for is a functional approach.

Questions

> Now, how can we understand this paradox?
> And why is this the case ...?
> And what does that mean?

Emphasis

> The main point I'd like to emphasise here is ...
> I should emphasize that ...
> There is, however, ONE aspect that ....
> The key issue is ...
> We should bear in mind that ...
> And / But the thing is ...
> I want to highlight ...

Clarifying

The points you make become much clearer to the listener if you

Paraphrase

> In other words, ...
> To put it differently, ...
> By which I mean ...
> ... in the sense that ...
> ... which means that ...

Spell out the implications

> These financial statements are standardized, **so** you can't put just anything in these reports
> This may constitute reparation in kind, **so if** ... then ... , **which means** ...
> If ... , **then this may indicate** that ...
> So **what I'm suggesting** is ...
> So **what I'm saying** is ...

Make the scope clearer by the use of contrast

> So, **in this sense** it is **different from** ...
> This might appear **contrary to** ... **but in fact** ....

Use an example

> For instance, ...
> A typical example of ...is ....
> So I've, got a slide here that **illustrates** how that works.
> So **suppose** we define E-of-S-C as the expected travel time.
> So **let's imagine** we're using P-P prime, you start with P.
> So, look at it this way, **suppose that** Dave and I are sellers and you're a buyer.
> **Say you** switch the temperature at this point to some other temperature T-S.

Stress the relevant word(s)

> No, although they DO want to improve this.
> I'm gonna go over just a couple of different areas that I haven't mentioned yet and teaching STYLE is one of them.

3.1 Rephrase the following sentences using a pseudo-cleft construction. Study the examples first.

We would also like to analyze why these dimensions are critical.
→ What we would like to do is <u>analyze why these dimensions are critical</u> (also stresses *analyze*)
→ What we would like to analyze is <u>why these dimensions are critical</u> (only stresses the object of analysis)

1. I'd like to <u>move on to the question of written assignments</u>.

2. I'm going to <u>describe briefly the main differences between English and German</u>.

3. I've tried to <u>put our recent difficulties into some kind of perspective</u>.

4. I'll be <u>making a case for getting in a team of specialists</u>.

5. So I'm saying that <u>this is a difficult issue</u>.

6. I'd like you to <u>ask yourselves a simple question</u>.

7. I'm going to be <u>looking at the arguments against networking</u>.

8. So I've <u>put together this flowchart</u>, as you can see.

9. You might <u>try to find a synonym</u>.

Note how speakers often repeat the introductory part of the sentence (as in sentence 2):

What I'm going to do is just briefly run through some of the main features.
What I'm going to do is I'm going to label these individually.

UNIT III

Referring to visuals

In the course of presentations or lectures, speakers often need to refer to visuals, such as graphs, figures or illustrations. In doing this, it is important not to get bogged down in details but to only highlight the aspects that are relevant to the rest of your talk.

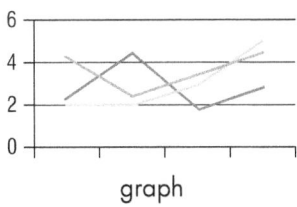
graph

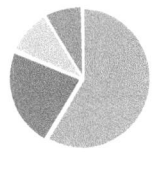
pie chart

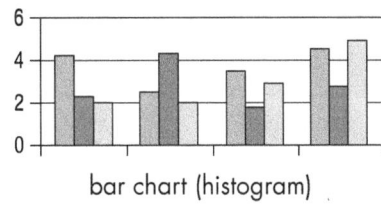
bar chart (histogram)

1. The language of graphics

1.1 Test your knowledge of graph language: Fill the gaps in the sentences below.

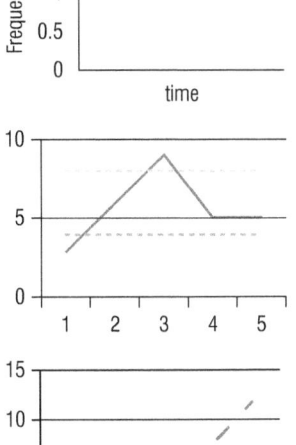

The **vertical a**................ represents frequency.

There are two **horizontal d**........... **lines**. The **lower one is** the baseline threshold. Then, **there's the upper line**, which is ...

Unlike the **s**............... **black line**, the **dashed line shows** a significant level of activity in the later stages of the cycle.

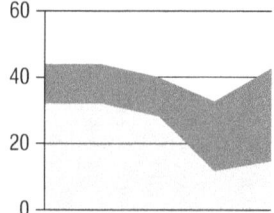

The **light grey s............. area indicates** the airflow range.

The following pages contain a range of commonly used expressions for referring to graphs and figures. A lot of vocabulary is field-specific, so it is useful to pay attention to the language used by other presenters in your field.

- LABELLING FEATURES

Typical verbs	Examples
represent indicate be have call label on / along the axis	Okay, so each column here **represents** an alpha. The X-axis **indicates** the data type. The Y-axis **is** the predicted temperature. In terms of our little diagram, **here we have** time. Why don't we just **call** this P? I'll **label** my axes X-one and X-two. The independent variable is **plotted on the horizontal axis**. **Along the X-axis is** the observed temperature

- HIGHLIGHTING POINTS OF INTEREST

Typical phrases	Examples
look at	Now **look at the red line**, which is the current situation. **Take a closer look at** this single data point.
see from	You **can see from the broken line that** … **As you could see from** the previous graph, …
show	Alright, **from this diagram here, you see that** …, right? The **second phase here shows** a more linear rate of settlement. The **next slide shows** the density patterns.
notice	**Now notice that** we have two P-K-A values And again **notice the area** around the neck of the sculpture.
point out	This is a really busy slide, so I'm **just going to point out** a few things on it. There's a couple of trends **I'd like to point out**.
focus	**I'd like you to focus on** the bottom part of the graph

- **PINPOINTING POSITION**
    > So that's the image **on the right side**.
    > There's one **on the left** and one below it.
    > That's what you're seeing on the screen, **over on the right**.
    > That is model two **in the right-hand column**.
    > If you look at the **upper left-hand corner** …
    > The **lower right** graph contains five axes.
    > That is what you can see **at the top of the diagram**.
    > The values of O-Factor and R-Factor are displayed **at the top** of the graph.
    > You notice there are zeros **in the top row**.
    > It's the **highest point** on the graph.
    > **At the bottom of the curve**, population is low.
    > So let's talk about line forty-five-oh-three, **along the bottom of the graph**.
    > if you look at the **bottom left of the graph**.
    > Firstly, look at the distribution of dots and blobs **above and below the quartile lines**.
    > Both lines meet **near the centre** of the graph.

Note the use of *this / these* … *(here)* to direct the audience's attention to a particular point of interest.
> I want you to concentrate on **these** blue Xs **here**.
> If you look at **this** point **here**, …

Sample texts

> In the **diagram that I'm showing you** there's – it's a growth trajectory, which you saw last time. There's a growth trajectory that **looks like this** right? And **this is** an ontogeny of how a particular species developed in the past, and that's an ancestor.
> Say, hypothetically, that the ancestor had two descendents, and one of those descendents had a longer growth rate, and one had a shorter growth rate, okay? **Here's the one with** the longer growth rate – that's descendent A – and **this is the one with** the shorter growth rate, with descendent B. (MICASE)

> The **decision table** has this piece over here which **is called** a condition stub, and this piece over here which **is called** the rule definition. And essentially all the condition stub and the rule definitions do, is ask a question and then give an exhaustive set of answers.
> Now what do i mean by an exhaustive set of answers? Well I'll deal with that in a moment. Finally, the **light-colored piece at the top** here, **describes** the problem space. The **piece at the bottom describes** what you're going to do, given certain conditions. And all they are is actions which you _ simply describe and then you check off under what conditions those actions are executed. (MICASE)

1.2 **Select the most appropriate verb for each sentence.**

DETERMINE – DIVERGE – SELECT – PLOT – CROSS

1. At this point, the two lines start to ....
2. These are the two points where the supply curve .... the demand curve.
3. This allows you to .... **the exact value** of temperature.
4. Since the n points are **randomly** .... from the set, these events are equally likely.
5. I've .... it **on** the FTSE100 chart for the last 6 months.

FLATTEN – HIT – FIT – MOVE – DECLINE

1. So, and the supply curve then .... the y axis.
2. As you can see, levels peak and then begin to .... quickly.
3. The rate increases very rapidly, initially, and then gradually .... **out**.
4. We'll just .... **down** to the bottom twenty percent now.
5. What type of curve would .... **the data** best?

1.3 **Insert prepositions.**

1. The clusters are distributed evenly **al**........... **the Y-axis**.
2. The two lines cross each other .... **this point**.
3. Also, the graph shows **a sharp drop** .... maximum wave-height.
4. Just **look** .... the top panel.
5. We have the probability that X is less than or **equal** .... Z.
6. Divide both sides .... point-eight then.
7. So I can **subtract** one equation .... the other?
8. **Multiply that** .... the square root of one.

> When using visuals, don't forget to check whether your audience can see them clearly.
>
> *Can you see the detail here?*
> *The dark line is a bit hard to see here, so let me write it on the board.*
> *Why don't you come over here, where you can see the screen, Philip?*
> *You might be able to see better from here.*

▶ *Referring to visuals*

2. Using numerals

■ CARDINAL NUMBERS

Pronunciation
> 0 zero/nought
> 100 a / one hundred
> 1,000 a / one thousand
> 1,000,000 a / one million
> 1,000,000,000 a /one billion

Use of *and* between hundreds and tens
> three hundred **and** sixty-five (British English)
> three hundred sixty five (American English)

■ DECIMALS

Decimals are marked by a "**.**"(*point*) in English.

- In mathematical contexts, where precision matters, the decimals are pronounced as separate digits.

  > 2.63 = two point six three
  > 18.589 = eighteen point five eight nine
  > 7.12% = seven point one two per cent

- In everyday conversation, people often pronounce decimals as a number.

  > 7.12% = seven point twelve per cent

- After the decimal point, 0 is read as 'oh'

  > 0.765 = zero / nought point seven six five
  > 6.705 = six point seven oh five

Speakers often prefer to round off numbers focus on significant trends. In doing so, they use approximations like *about* or *almost*.

> As you can see, insulin control accounts for **about 25 percent** of your brain function.

2.1 **Highlight all approximations in the sentences below.**

1. Nearly half of this population suffers from symptoms of burnout.
2. The bar for 2001 reaches to just under 40%.
3. And you'll see here that, as you go up in the basin, that the elevation increases from approximately nine hundred meters to almost two thousand meters.
4. The chart on my next slide shows that just over half of all respondents reported ....

5. Roughly speaking, about fifty percent of all lupus patients will develop this nephritis.
6. The graph climbs from roughly 10 percent to 25 percent between 2000 and 2008.
7. But, after all, the sun makes up some 99 percent of the solar system.

UNIT IV

Delivery

1. Speaking to your audience

Read the email below, which was sent to participants in the run-up to a conference. Do you agree with the advice given?

> **Reading aloud at conferences[3]**
> Many conference presenters, particularly in the USA, prefer to read their papers aloud. While there is a long tradition of reading aloud at some academic conferences, particularly where the presenters are researchers and not teachers, this technique also has several drawbacks and we would like to discourage it at EATAW for the following reasons:
> - The **syntax** of written language is different from that of speech: while oral syntax is simple, assuming an audience with a limited attention span grasping at a transient message, written syntax is much denser and more complex, assuming an audience which is at liberty to read and re-read a permanent message. Several non-native-speaker members (we remind presenters that the majority of EATAW members are neither native speakers nor English teachers) at our last conference complained that they had difficulty in following the ideas of native speakers who read aloud.
> - Unless one is very experienced or has training, it is hard to read aloud in a way that sounds like natural speech. With the best will in the world, the reader's voice typically becomes **flat and unnatural**, with a tendency to 'drone on'. Little is better calculated to send an audience to sleep than this, regardless of how valuable and groundbreaking the content may be.
> - Reading aloud, because of the need to constantly refer to the text on the lectern, severely reduces **eye contact** between speaker and audience. Not only is it difficult for the reader, preoccupied with his/her own text, to pick up on visual feedback and accordingly explain, slow down or recap, but the audience, deprived of speaker eye-contact, feel cut off from what is going on. We would like to maximise the possibility at EATAW for two way communication.

---

3. Email sent to EATAW conference mailing list (European Association for the Teaching of Academic Writing).

> *Some non-native speakers prefer reading aloud because the text can be prepared in advance, thus reducing nervousness. We understand this concern very well, however, given the choice between a safe, boring talk that may alienate the audience and a more risky talk that may interest them at the danger of making some small slips or nervous errors, we hope most presenters would choose the latter. We would like to reassure nervous non- native presenters that their audience, being in large part composed of other non-native speakers, will be sympathetic and supportive to those who feel insecure about presenting in a foreign language.*
>
> *We appreciate that many of you may already be quite comfortable with presentation skills. If so, please ignore this message. For those who feel less familiar or comfortable with presentation skills, we are preparing a page of tips and suggestions on how to give a good presentation without reading aloud, which will shortly be available at: http://www.ceu.hu/eataw/dontread.htm*
>
> *With best wishes,*
>
> *John Harbord*
> *EATAW Conference Organiser*

- ■ POINTS TO KEEP IN MIND
- It is easier to keep your audience's attention if you are speaking to them rather than reading to them.
- If you are using PowerPoint, avoid reading from the screen.
- If you do decide to read your paper, because this is most common in your discipline, additional preparation will be required to make the text suitable for a spoken register and to practise a lively intonation.
- Some speakers opt for a compromise solution, speaking naturally in some parts and reading from their notes in others, but this is actually not such a good idea: your audience will switch off as soon as you start reading.
- Whether or not you read your text aloud, a lively intonation and good eye contact are essential in involving the audience. In addition, occasionally referring to the audience (*as you may know*) or to yourself (*I'll explain about that in a minute*) will also help create a rapport, because it shows that you are aware of being "in the moment" rather than wrapped up in your text.

- ■ COMMON PROBLEMS

Intonation

- **Flat, monotonous intonation**: it is very hard to read a text aloud in a lively, natural manner, but also when improvising many presenters speak monotonously, due to a lack of confidence or because their habitual speaking style is fairly low-key. If this is the case, try to emphasise key words more and to convey interest and enthusiasm.

- **"Sing-song" intonation**: this will make you sound over-rehearsed and out of touch with your audience. Aim for a more natural, conversational style.

- **Rising intonation**: if your tone goes up towards the end of the sentence, all your statements will sound like questions. This will make you come across as insecure.

- **Over-emphatic intonation**: some parts of the presentation should be fairly emphatic, for instance the introduction or major transitions, but if this style is kept up the whole time, the audience may find it rather exhausting, so alternate with more low-key, conversational passages.

- **Foreign intonation patterns**: it is often hard to get rid of the intonation patterns of your own language, which may impede comprehension. If this is the case, try not to speak too quickly. Speaking in a relaxed manner will help you to get your message across better.

Eye contact

- **Lack of eye contact**: if you continuously look at the ceiling, at your notes or at the slides projected on the wall, this will make it hard to involve the audience, because you come across as wrapped up in yourself. If you are nervous about making eye contact, focus on people's foreheads or look in between faces.

- **Partial eye contact**: many presenters unconsciously focus on one side of the room, so remember to look around regularly. If part of the audience is blocked from view (e.g. by the overhead projector), change position now and then.

- **Too much eye contact**: it is important to maintain good eye contact, but it will make people nervous if you stare at them.

Pace

- **Pace too fast**: if the pace is too fast, the audience does not have time to absorb the information that is presented and the presentation becomes less effective. Try to speak in a relaxed manner and insert enough pauses throughout your talk. Speeding up is often related to poor timing, so make sure your presentation fits the time slot. If you are worried that you tend to speak too fast, try out your presentation in advance and ask someone for feedback.

- **Pace too slow**: sometimes presenters speak too hesitantly; this is often due to lack of preparation.

2. Chunking and emphasis

Speech is not a continuous stream of sound: it is made up of « chunks » of words pronounced in the same breath, with shorter and longer pauses in between.

For example

> **one** of the issues that I want to **concentrate** on today /
> is the issue of the linguistic **impact** of **language contact** //
> one of the main **themes** that I've been **stressing** /
> throughout the last couple of **classes** /
> has been that in the linguistic **history** of the region /...

Good chunking, with emphasis on the key words, is a very important speaking skill, because it underlines the meaning of what you are saying, thus facilitating understanding.

- COMMON PROBLEMS

- **Lack of pauses between chunks**: this is more likely to happen if you read your text aloud, but even when speaking naturally many presenters have a fairly rapid pace. In order to improve this, you simply need to insert slightly longer pauses, to punctuate the stream of words. If you hear yourself speeding up, a useful trick is to mentally count one or two seconds between your sentences. This is especially important at transitions, where the pauses should be longer. For instance, a signpost like *"the second point is"* will lose much of its effect if it follows the preceding sentence without any interruption.

- **Too many short chunks:** short chunks of 2 or 3 words are very effective to give your main points additional emphasis, but if you do this all the time your style will lack fluency (e.g. *This is / undoubtedly / the single / most important / contribution / in the last decade*).

- **Faulty chunking**: it is important to segment in a meaningful way, as pausing in the middle of a meaningful unit will make what you say much harder to interpret for the listener and may even create ambiguity, as the following examples illustrate.

    > *He was invited to attend a seminar on peace / in Jerusalem.*
    > *He was invited to attend a seminar / on peace / in Jerusalem.*

    > *What these children need is more homework guidance / and orientation.*
    > *What these children need is more homework / guidance / and orientation.*

- **Lack of emphasis**: if you stress all words evenly, the meaning may be unclear. Use emphasis to bring your message across.

- **Faulty emphasis**: within the chunk, the main stress tends to come at the end, but contrastive stress may be placed on any word in the chunk. Practise your text well: if you are insufficiently aware of the sentence that follows, you may find yourself stressing the wrong word.

    one of the main ***themes*** that I've been ***stressing***
    one of the main ***themes*** that ***I've*** been stressing (in contrast to the previous presenter)

3. Guidelines for visuals

- POWERPOINT PRESENTATIONS
- Limit the amount of text on a slide: standard advice is to use no more than seven lines per slide and seven words per line, so condense sentences into brief phrases that you will elaborate.
    - Your audience should be able to process the information quickly.
    - Your slides should not contain your entire presentation: if everything you say is on the slide, your audience does not need to listen to you.
- To be legible, it is usually recommended that the font should be 24pt or larger.
- Use colours and animation effects sparingly: ornate templates and excessive use of visual effects will tend to annoy your audience.
- Use parallelism in bulleted lists
- Don't forget to check your slides for spelling errors.

3.1 Improve parallelism in the following slide:

Aims

The aim of the workshop is threefold
- ☐ to showcase our research
- ☐ providing an overview of ongoing projects
- ☐ the role of external partners

- POSTER PRESENTATIONS
- Design your poster with a strolling crowd in mind. Try to make it as attractive as possible.
- Make your title clear and prominent so viewers can identify your paper easily.
- Use lay-out and headings to help readers find key sections at a glance (e.g. objectives, result).
- Column format makes poster easier to read in a crowd.
- State your main points as succinctly as possible: It is generally advised to keep text elements to 50 words or less. Remove anything that is not essential to your main message. Use phrases rather than full sentences.
- Text should be large – use at least 36 point for title panels; 24 point for text.
- Graphs should be simple and clean.
- Use a light colour background and dark letters for contrast. Avoid dark background with light letters, as this is very tiring to read.

4. Practice makes perfect

It is important to practise your presentation several times.

- If you intend to read a fully written text, it is important to be thoroughly familiar with it, so that you can pause in the right places, speak with a more natural intonation and have at least some eye contact with your audience.
- If you intend to improvise from notes that contain only the key ideas, rehearsing will enable you to speak much more fluently: even if the wording is slightly different each time, the right words and phrases will come to you much more easily. A handy tip: if you use cards rather than sheets of paper, the audience won't notice that your hands are trembling slightly.
- Rehearsing will help you become aware of structural and stylistic problems: you will notice if a passage is too long, or if a transition or interpolation seems to take you off track, or if a sentence structure is too complex.
- Practising the use of visuals will help you seem more in control.
- Timing your practice sessions will give you an idea of the presentation's actual length. If it is too long, do not speed up, but cut the less important passages: you can always refer to these when answering questions.

Part Two

Interacting with Colleagues and Students

UNIT I

Handling the question-and-answer session

Presenters usually feel least comfortable with the question-and-answer session, when they can't entirely rely on preparation. Similarly, members of the audience may feel at a disadvantage to native speakers in formulating questions and comments. This unit provides help in these areas.

1. Asking questions

Research shows that in seminars the questions asked by non-native speakers are generally shorter and more abrupt than those asked by native speakers. The following pages suggest ways of making your contributions less direct.

- META-STATEMENTS

Questions and comments are often introduced by a phrase that indicates explicitly that a question will be asked or an objection raised. Try to avoid bluntness, as shown in some of the examples below.

I want to ask a question ...	→	*I just wanted to ask you...* *I would just like to ask whether...* *I have a question (about ...)*
There's something I don't understand ...	→	*I'm not sure I understood you correctly. Could you...*
I don't agree	→	*I'm not entirely convinced that ...*
I want to add something	→	*I just have a comment* *I would just like to share a comment*

1.1 Underline the meta-statements in the following sentences and indicate how the message has been softened.

1. You didn't, <u>I believe</u>, talk about the syntactic differences among adjectives; I didn't hear that anyway.
2. <u>I was wondering</u> if you had done any applications of this or if you are thinking of coming up with applications.
3. Yes, <u>I was just going to ask you</u> if there's any way of knowing the gender of …
4. <u>Just something to share</u>, when I was in Iran in the seventies there was…
5. <u>I'm curious</u>; in the context of the lecture, does the audience – especially juveniles – do they tend to ask questions or not at the end?
6. Yes, <u>I just wondered</u> about the status of your letter because the mission statements are probably documents, so you can cite them.
7. <u>I've got a question.</u> I'd like to know how this relates to the fact that certain steps are optional in the macrostructure of the genres.

1.2 Insert *just* or *quite* to make the following statements sound less direct.

1. I don't understand what the point of your example from Beowulf is.
2. Could I ask you on the Carbon Trust, what is your responsibility for that? We are not clear which department is responsible for it.
3. I'd like to point out that …
4. Could I make a point about …
5. I'm afraid I'm not clear what you mean by that.
6. Remind me: what was the third category again?
7. Can I say that I thought your analysis of the situation was excellent.
8. What exactly does this do? I'm sorry but I don't get your point.
9. One thing worries me about your results.
10. Sorry, but I don't see what you mean. Could you explain that last bit again?

> Note how progressive forms make the message more tentative
>
> I was just wondering if maybe I missed that.
> I was just going to ask whether …
> So basically what you're saying is that …
> Are you suggesting that ….
> That's not really what I was asking.

■ MORE EXAMPLES

Asking for clarification and further information

> *I'm sorry, I didn't quite follow what you said about ...*
> *I'm afraid I didn't get your last point. Could you go over it again, please?*
> *I'm sorry but could you explain in a little more detail?*
> *Could you elaborate on that?*
> *Have you taken ... into account?*
> *Can you think of any reason why ...*

Asking for confirmation

> *So, if I understand you correctly, you're saying that ...*
> *Am I correct in assuming that ...*
> *Would I be correct in saying that ...*

Introducing a comment

> *I wonder if I could comment on that last point ...*
> *I'd like to add something here if I may ...*
> *Before we go any further, may I point out that ...*

Formulating an objection

> *Wouldn't you agree that ...*
> *I'm not really convinced that ...*
> *On what basis do you ...?*
> *But isn't it really a question of ...*
> *But surely ...*
> *It seems to me that ...*
> *I just wondered if ...*

■ ELABORATION

Questions that are too short and to the point may sound aggressive. Possible strategies for avoiding this are:

Referring back to what the speaker said as a lead-in to your question.

> *Going back to the first part of the presentation, I wanted to ask, you seem to make a distinction between ...*

Paraphrasing or refining your question

> *You'd have to have an a priori proof of that without knowing what the commands were, right? I mean without knowing what the principles were. (MICASE)*

Spelling out implications / asking for confirmation

Are you suggesting that – in the last few minutes of your talk you said the church should look at different it appeared to me that you were saying different models of relationships and so forth. – are you saying that ... (MICASE)

Formulating a statement or hypothesis on which you ask the speaker's view

I wonder, and this is hardly a response to you, just the statement you just gave, if you might not have a rise in biodiversity when you move from the forest. (MICASE)

Wouldn't it be simpler just to say that ...

Giving reasons for your question

Um, is there any training or any work being done with the faculty, because you just mentioned you are doing that with foreign students coming in.

First thanking the speaker for the talk

That was a very interesting paper, thank you. I like this idea of the mandated genre. But another term that you use ...

1.3 **Below are some more examples of such more elaborate questions: add useful phrases to the box.**

I have a question about old sciences vs. new sciences. I was wondering how much of the evolution of education and careerism in traditional sciences, such as physics, are affected by what seems to be exponential (even explosive) growth in new sciences, such as information sciences, computer sciences, etc.[4]

Could you go into more detail on the problems with the peer review process? Are you saying that there is evidence that the current process is flawed, showing flaws, or soon will?[5]

You mentioned your role as a G-7 Deputy. Currently, the G-7 is pushing the IMF to charge higher interest rates for long-term borrowers, specifically in regard to relations of borrowers to private-sector lenders. Do you think this is necessary and how would this happen? Will it happen?[6]

---

4. From www.marshall.org.
5. Idem.
6. From www.imf.org/external.

1.4 *When you were ...* : Fill the gaps.

1. When you were .... **with** lexicographical typologies, you c..................... **on** the complex task of matching dictionaries to the typological scheme. Could you **e**..................... **on** that?
2. When you were .... **about** Raymond Carver earlier, you **r**..................... **to** the Beef Trust. Could you .... **us a little more** about that?
3. When you were **de**..................... the Swedish model, you **s**..................... **that** without male demand there would be no female supply. I **w**..................... **if** this is not somewhat utopian.
4. When you were **de**..................... Cholesky factorizations, you **m**..................... **that** total number of FLOPs decreases by a factor of approximately 4 in going down one tree level. Could you **ex**..................... this **in some more** ...., or perhaps .... **an example**?
5. When you were **di**..................... juvenile delinquents, you **made the** .... **that** some feel that too much affluence can lead to aimlessness and delinquency. Could you **be more** .... about that?

1.5 Fill the gaps.

1. **I have a question** .... the possible effects of other uncontrolled variables.
2. What .... do you mean by a "calculated risk"?
3. Could we **go** .... what you were saying about polymers?
4. How did you .... **at** the figure of £1000 for the base level?
5. If I **understood** you ...., what you are .... saying is that ischemia causes white cell activation. Is that right?
6. I'm not sure I .... **understood**. Can you **run through** that again, please?
7. There's one thing **I'm not** .... **about**. Could you **go over** that again, please?
8. You use the word *redemptive* several times. Could you **expand** .... the word *redemptive*?

1.6 Rearrange the alphabetical lists into meaningful sentences

could
elaborate
on   } Could you elaborate on that?
that
you

1.	2.	3.	4.	5.
afraid	clear	another	do	could
am	didn't	it	exactly	I
don't	I	let	issue	later
follow	make	me	on	on
I	myself	put	stand	perhaps
I	perhaps	way	this	point
quite			where	return
			you	that
				to

6.	7.	8.	9.	10.
comment	don't	as	am	a
could	head	as	clear	am
I	I	don't	I	but
I	know	I	mean	could
if	my	it's	not	detail
last	of	quite	on	explain
on	off	simple	quite	I
point	that	that	what	in
that	the	think	you	little
wonder	top			more
				sorry
				you

2. Responding to questions and objections

Thanking the questioner

That's a very interesting question.
I'm glad you asked that question.
You've raised an important point there.
I see where you're going and I think that's a really good point.

Asking clarification

It depends what you mean by …
I'm not quite sure what you mean by that.
I'm afraid I don't quite follow.
Would you repeat the question?

Evading the question

I'm afraid I don't have information at my disposal to answer that.
I think we can leave the problem of … aside for a moment; the real issue is …
But I know this isn't a totally satisfactory way to respond.

Rephrasing

Perhaps I haven't made myself clear. Basically, what I'm trying to say is …
Sorry, I'm probably not making myself clear. Let me put it another way …
Perhaps I should make that clearer by saying …
To be more specific, …
Put simply …
What I meant was …
Let me put it another way …
What I'm trying to say is …
Let me rephrase what I just said …

Checking

Is this making sense?
(Does) that make sense?
Do you see what I'm saying?
See?
Okay?
Right?

Coming back to a point

So, as I was saying …
Coming back to what I was saying …
To return to …
Perhaps I could return to that point later on.
Your question leads us back to …
As I said, one of the problems that we have right now, today, is that …

Giving an opinion

In my view / opinion (NOT: *according to me)
In my experience …
I'd say that …
I would argue that …
As far as I can tell …
It seems to me that …
Personally, my feeling is that …
My impression is that …

Responding tactfully to critical questions

Well yes, I suppose so.
That's one way of looking at it, but …
Yes, possibly, but …
Not necessarily.
Well, you have a point there, but …
Personally, I wouldn't go so far as to say that ..
I take your point, but …
What you say is largely true. Nevertheless, I do not think that …

2.1 Make the following statements more indirect. Try various alternatives.

1. It's not as bad as that →

2. It's not as simple as that →

3. [Do you agree?] No →

4. The second factor is more important →

5. I want to get back to the conclusion →

Handling the question-and-answer session

> ▢ Note the frequent use of adverbs like *basically*, *definitely*, and *exactly* in formulating points and questions.
>
> *So basically you could say that …*
> *So basically, um what kinds of consequences are there?*
>
> *I mean, I think it definitely has a lot to do with …*
> *That's definitely a good example of how …*
>
> *That is exactly what I meant when I said …*
> *What exactly does that mean again?*

2.2 Fill the gaps with an appropriate word.

1. I'm ……………… I don't see the connection.
2. Can I **get** ……………… **to you on** that?
3. Well, ……………… I said earlier, …
4. To be honest, I think that **raises** a different ………………
5. That's not something I've had time to ……………… **with**, but …
6. Well, **to be** ………………, I'm not really the right person to ask about that.
7. Sorry, could I ……………… finish?
8. Perhaps I didn't **make myself** ……………… What I was trying to say was …
9. Anyway, I will ……………… **it there for now**.

2.3 Add the correct prepositions.

1. That's a good point, actually. so let's let's **keep** that …………… **mind**.
2. To **get back** …………… what I was saying …
3. …………… **first glance** it looks as if that is the case, but in fact …
4. I don't know that …………… **the top of my head**.
5. That's an interesting point. I'm glad you **brought** that ……………
6. Right, I see what you're **getting** …………… And of course …
7. …………… **the whole**, yes, but there are other factors involved.
8. …………… **the best of my knowledge**, this has not been investigated yet.
9. That **depends** …………… what you mean by *transcendent*.
10. Right, if there are no other questions, perhaps we should **wrap** it …………… here?

📝 Interjections and discourse markers are often hard to translate. English typically uses question tags or markers such as *well, so* or *right*:

*That's interesting, **è**.*	>	*That's interesting, **isn't it**?*
*You knew that, **è**.*	>	*You knew that, **didn't you**?*
***Enfin**, that brings us to our next point.*	>	***Right**, that brings us to our next point.*
***Allez**, I don't think so.*	>	***Well**, I don't think so.*
***Oei**, I just dropped this.*	>	***Oops**, I just dropped this.*

UNIT II
Chairing a conference session

1. Guidelines for chairing

- Prior to the session, contact the conference organizers to know what is expected of you.
- Go to the room well in advance to meet with speakers and check that equipment is functioning.
- Tell speakers what signal you will use to notify them that their time is nearly up (e.g. cue cards).
- For each talk, introduce the speaker, give their affiliation and the title of their talk. Lengthy introductions are only appropriate for keynote speakers or leading authorities in the field.
  > Our next speaker is Mike Wald, from Southampton University. He'll be talking about Personalized Displays.
- Ensure that each session starts and finishes on time. Remind speakers if necessary.
- Take charge of the question time:
  - invite questions from the audience
  - have a question ready to get the discussion off the ground
  - intervene if one person dominates the discussion
  - wrap up the discussion and thank the speaker

1.1 Fill the gaps.

Preparing the session

1. Can everyone **see cl**..........................?
2. You're **blocking the v**...................... this way.
3. There's a **r**...................... (*electronic device to switch to your next slide*) available if you would like to use one.
4. I will show you a **cue c**...................... with a five-minute announcement, and one which says you have one more minute to go.

Introducing the next speaker

1. Our **f**...................... (*last*) **speaker** today is ..., who will talk about ...
2. We've had a complication with our first speaker due to travel miscommunication. She will be here **sh**...................... . Until that time we'd like to have a **10-15 minute rec**...................... (*break*). I do ask that you all be back here in ten minutes or so.
3. Welcome indeed. Then we have Dr Jesus Ramones. Is that the right **pro**...................... ?
4. Am I **pro**...................... this correctly?

Addressing problems during the presentation

1. Could you perhaps **speak a little l**.................... ? The people at the back can't hear you.
2. Could you **speak u**................. a little?
3. Hmm, the screen's **gone bl**.................... . Let me just find someone to fix this.

Ensuring a speaker stays within the allocated time limits

1. I'm afraid I really have to **cut you sh**.................... here, as we need to allow time for questions.
2. I'm sorry, we really have to stop now; we're **r**...................... **out of time**.

Starting the Q & A session

1. I do not know who would like to **k**........... **off**. Mr Ash, perhaps?
2. I am **s**.................... you will have many questions.
3. OK, we have **ab**.................... fifteen minutes for questions and discussion. Would **a**...................... like to start?
4. We have **s**.................... **more time**.
5. We actually have **pl**.................... **of time** for discussion.

Moderating and ending the Q & A sessions

1. OK, there, 2nd row .... **the back**.
2. Here .... **my left**.
3. I think there are other people .... have questions.
4. There're other people that had their hand up, so let's **go to** .... else and then we can circle back to you when other people have **had a** .... to speak.
5. Sorry to **c**.................... **you short**, but I'm hoping to **move** .... **to** the next part of the debate.

6. Okay, one last question before we **wr**.................... this **up**.
7. I think we have time for one last question before we **br**.................... for lunch.

> ### Someone or anyone?
>
> **Somebody / someone** is used:
> - in affirmative sentences
>   *Let's go to somebody else first.*
>
> - in requests and offers (when you expect the answer to be yes)
>   *Could somebody close that window?*
>
> **Anybody / anyone** is used:
> - in negative sentences and after words like *never, without, hardly* ...
>   *I don't think anybody has ever measured the difference.*
>
> - in questions
>   *We have about 15 minutes for questions. Would anyone like to start?*

2. Introducing a plenary speaker

- GUIDELINES
- Consider carefully what information your introduction should contain: do not simply read a list of achievements but try to highlight why the speaker's work and expertise is relevant to the audience.

- Keep your introduction short and do not cover the speaker's ground by elaborating on the topic.

- Praise should sound genuine, so avoid clichés as far as possible (e.g. *Our next speaker needs no introduction*).

- It is not a good idea to rely on improvisation, so prepare your text carefully, but do not read it aloud as this may make the introduction sound perfunctory. Make sure your tone is warm and welcoming.

SAMPLE TEXTS

> *Our next speaker is Katherine L. Cousins. Kate is chair of the Committee on Technology, which is made up of nine prominent leaders of science and technology. It is their job to dig into all of our institute's obscure corners and tell us what we are doing right and where we have "room for improvement." Believe me, they love the "room for improvement" part. Seriously, we appreciate their advice and counsel and take it to heart. In addition to her role as chair of the committee, Kate is a scientist who has worked in the chemical industry for 30 years in a number of increasingly responsible positions, including vice president at Water Products and Chemicals. Currently, she is president of the Council for Technological Research. It is my pleasure to introduce Kate Cousins.*

It is a particular pleasure for me today to introduce our honored speaker, Professor Gary Glick, who is Professor of Chemistry and Professor of Biological Chemistry, and who was named to the Werner E Bachmann Collegiate Professorship of Chemistry in 1999.

Gary Glick **received a** BA **degree from** Rutgers University in 1983, and a PhD degree from Columbia in 1988. **He joined** the University of Michigan's Department of Chemistry in 1990, and **is now widely regarded as a major figure in the area of** Chemical Biology. Professor Glick has combined research expertise in organic chemistry and in structural biochemistry, a combination which enables him to solve important problems in medicine and biological systems.

His record reflects accomplishments in two distinct lines of research. First he has developed synthetic and physical methods to critical questions of nucleic acid structure, dynamics and folding. And second, he has established an understanding of the molecular basis for the recognition of DNA by pathogenic anti-DNA antibodies characteristic of the autoimmune disorder systemic erythematosus.

The two lines of research carried out by Doctor Glick are quite independent, and they require different techniques, skills, insights and knowledge sets. Very few scientists can bring such diverse skills and technology to bear on scientific issues, and **his achievements in this have already been recognized by numerous awards and honors**. He received a National Science Foundation Young Investigator Award, a Junior Faculty Research Award from the American Cancer Society, a National Arthritis Foundation Investigator Award, a Camille Dreyfuss Teacher Scholar Award, and an appointment as a Research Follow of the Alfred P Sloan Foundation.

He is a co-principal investigator on the NIH funded Chemistry Biology Training Grant at the University of Michigan and he has served as an ad hoc member of the Bio-organic Chemistry Study section of the NIH, as well as assuming the position of co-editor of Current Protocols, and Nucleic Acid Chemistry. This, I have to say, is an outstanding career for somebody ten years out of the end of his post-doctoral fellowship.

> *In addition to being* an outstanding researcher, doctor Glick is a dynamic and very effective teacher, who **has contributed a great deal to** the development of a new curriculum in chemical biology at the graduate level. Doctor Glick's ability to **excel as a teacher** while developing and rapidly **making highly significant contributions** in two distinct lines of research, all within a few years of initiating his own independent research program, is remarkable.
>
> His accomplishments are clear and compelling, and his promise for the future truly exceptional. He's clearly one of the best minds in chemistry of his generation. **I am very happy to present to you today** Professor Gary D Glick, whose lecture in entitled Research and Discovery at the Interface of Chemistry, Biology, and Medicine. **A short question and answer period will follow the lecture**, after which you're invited to join all of us, including doctor Glick, and to have conversation with doctor Glick in the assembly hall, which is located straight through these doors, and across the corridor. (MICASE)

- USEFUL PHRASES

Skim the sample texts above for additional phrases

Introductory phrase

> *It gives me great pleasure to introduce …*
> *… a friend, former colleague and distinguished figure in the field of …*
> *It is my pleasure to introduce …*
> *… has kindly agreed to speak to us on the subject of*
> ....
> ....
> ....

Qualifications

> *received her (degree) from …*
> *holds honorary degrees from …*
> *She has held a series of positions in …*
> ....
> ....
> ....

Achievements and publications

> *… is a much published authority in*
> *… has disseminated her work in several papers presented at*
> ....
> ....
> ....

Ending

> I asked ... to talk to is about ... . No one is more suited for this task.
> I am pleased to present ....

....
....
....

2.1 **Circle the correct verb forms.**

1. He *received / has received* his Ph.D. in mathematics from Princeton in 1962.
2. Since then, he *took / has taken* a high profile role on several major projects.
3. He *published / has published* widely on international and community law.
4. Last year he *was / has been* elected Fellow of the British Academy.
5. Prior to his studies at the University of London, he *spent / has spent* a year at Warwick.
6. These questions *became / have become* increasingly prominent in academic debate over the last decade.

> When describing the speaker's career, generally the SIMPLE PAST is used, especially with past time reference:
> ... **received** her B.S. from Warwick in 1963
> Over the following two decades he **led** ...
> Prior to her appointment at ... , she **was** ...
> Following this, he **served** as ...
> but: She'**s been** William Dunn Professor of Biochemistry since 1995 (still going on).
>
> Use the PRESENT PERFECT to stress achievements:
> She **has held** a series of positions in ...
> He **has published** widely on ...
> but: She **won** the Baird Award in 1999 (at a specific time).
>
> The PRESENT SIMPLE is used for current positions or facts:
> ... **is** currently Professor of ...
> ... **is** an authority in the field of ...
>
> Use the PRESENT CONTINUOUS for ongoing activities:
> ... **is writing** a book about ...

▶ *Chairing a conference session*

2.2 **Correct errors in the following sentences.**

1. This is the topic where she works on.
2. He currently writes a thesis titled...
3. Her main interests are concerned about ...
4. More specific, she is studying the effects of ...
5. I'm very pleased to present you Antonio Jimenez.

Do NOT use the following phrases
   * I give the word to ....
   * The word is to ...

Instead, say something like this:
   Ladies and gentlemen, please welcome X.
   Please join me in welcoming ...
   I am pleased to present X.

Or simply mention the presenter's name again.
   Ladies and gentlemen: Sybil Waldorf.

---

3. Thanking a speaker

I want to thank Bob Stinnett for taking the time to join us, and also for the really remarkable work that he's done. I mean, this has been an effort that others have attempted to do, and there's still a lot to be learned, obviously, not just about Pearl Harbor but about many other aspects of government policy. That's a lot of what the Independent Institute is involved in, so I think Bob deserves our special thanks for the work he's done in producing this book.

Dr. Goodstein, we'd like to thank you for your very interesting presentation and discussion of this issue.

On your behalf, I would like to thank Mr. Nick Scheele most sincerely, for accepting our invitation to give this Lecture and for providing us all, with a stimulating and visionary presentation which I know, from the buzz which I detected afterwards, will leave a lasting impression on all here, tonight. He has certainly given me food for thought.

Are there other questions to Professor Glick...? Well if not it falls to me on your behalf to thank, Gary Glick for a talk that clearly was full of scientific interest to judge from your questions, asked from a base of expertise somewhat greater than my own and also to thank him for doing such important work whether or not we are scientists, any of us who have had any contact with individuals who have lupus, will understand what an important piece of research this is to some of our fellow human beings. Thank you very much, Gary, for a splendid lecture. (MICASE)

3.1 Cull useful phrases from the excerpts above.

UNIT III

Tutoring students

1. Giving instructions

Instructions can be given in various ways, ranging from more to less direct.

Present tense

Simple present tenses are often used to explain procedures. Also, note the frequent use of pseudo-cleft structures (*what you do is you ...*) in such contexts.

> *So you take one of those pluses away and then what you do is you add two minuses.*
> *So, you first start at node two and you follow all the paths going out of node two.*
> *What you do is you take the derivative and set it equal to zero.*

Please

Please followed by infinitive expresses a command, so it is used for instructions and invitations but not for polite requests or tentative suggestions.

> *Please take a look at what these words actually mean.*
> *Please rate these sentences on a scale of one to five.*
> *Please take a form and pass it around.*
> *Please remember to turn in your sheets.*
> *Please feel free to send them to me.*
> *Would someone please read this passage?*

I want you to ...

I want you to ... or *I would like you to ...* is typically used in classroom contexts rather than in one-to-one interaction.

> *I want you to concentrate on these blue Xs here.*
> *I want you to go back to chapter two and read page forty-seven to fifty-one.*
> *What I want you to remember is it's one of many theories.*
> *I would like you to remember those three terms.*
> *I would like you to read the questions.*

Let's ... / let me ...

Sentences with *let's* or *let me* are mainly used to mark transitions or to invite requests for help or clarification (*let me know ...*).

> *Let's start with question number one, read it through, and ask me questions.*
> *Okay, let's tally our results and see, empirically, what the answers should be.*
> *Let me just add this here then.*
> *Let me know when you come across terms or concepts that you don't know.*

Why don't you ... ?

Why don't you is typically used for invitations, for instance to invite students to respond or participate.

> *Jeremy, why don't you start and tell us what your thoughts were about this?*
> *Why don't you grab a chair somewhere and join us?*
> *Why don't you talk a little about what your focus was?*
> *Why don't you come over here where you can see the computer*
> *Why don't you take another film and video course then?*

Instructing students to pay attention

> *Could I have your attention, please?*
> *OK, pay attention to the screen now!*

2. Making suggestions

Suggestions are usually more tentative than direct instructions. For this reason, the verb *suggest* itself is actually not often used to make suggestions, particularly in spoken language, as *I suggest that* sounds quite formal and distant. This may be suitable for fairly anonymous instructions, but not for one-to-one interaction.

> *I **suggest** that you check the websites of the universities that you're interested in.*
> *I **suggest** that this report should be about 10 pages long.*
> *Unless you have some previous experience, I would **suggest** that you take the MPhil course rather than start a PhD straightaway.*

Note how suggest is often toned down by the use of a modal verb. This use is still highly formal, however.

> *I **would suggest** that you limit your search by date.*
> *If so, then I **might suggest** you take this course instead.*
> ***May I suggest** that you try contacting the Secretary?*

Below, the most typical ways of formulating suggestions in spoken language are described.

- STRONG SUGGESTIONS

Should

Should is used for fairly strong suggestions, in which the speaker speaks with authority

> One thing that you **should** be aware of is that you can't double-count courses
> That's why you **should** always build two models.
> That's probably something you **should** be thinking about

Need

Need presents the suggestion as a necessity. This is often made more tentative by the use of words such as *may* or *probably*.

> Okay, now, what you **need** to do is consider both sides.
> One thing you **need** to be cautious of is that this can overestimate the speed of response.
> That's **maybe** the direction you **need** to go in.
> You **may need** to correct your data.
> You will **probably need** to think about this.

I would / wouldn't ...

People often give advice by saying what they *would* or *wouldn't* do if they were in the listener's position. Note that if you use an if-clause, you should not use *would* after if (so not: *if I would ...*).

> If I were to rephrase this, I **would** say something like ...
> What I **would** do here is to insert quotations.
> I probably **wouldn't** use that word.
> I **wouldn't** rewrite the whole paper.
> I think it **would** be more interesting to combine these approaches.

You (might) want to ...

Fairly strong suggestions are often expressed by a form of *you want*. This is used when the advice is pretty straightforward and not really debatable. (e.g. *You will want to turn left at the next traffic lights*). Modal verbs (e.g. *might, would*) are often added to tone down the suggestion.

> You **want** a really good solid basis in general chemistry before going on to organic.
> These are classes you **don't want** to miss.

> You **wouldn't want** to take two history courses and two political science courses together.
> You **might want** to highlight that distinction
> So, you **might want** to think about German and Russian.
> If you have a problem, you **will want** to go to the PECS office and talk to them.

- MORE TENTATIVE SUGGESTIONS AND INVITATIONS

Could / Might

The use of *could* or *might* is less direct, as it presents the suggestion as an option to be considered.

> Another thing that you **could** do is to take an Anthropology course.
> You **could** also put this in the body of the email.
> What you **could** do is try to create a community.
> That's something that you **might** think about.
> You **might be interested in a book by … on this topic**.
> It **might** be worth mentioning one of those points. [note the use of the gerund after 'worth']

Hedging

As was pointed out above, advice is often made more 'palatable' by the use of tentative language (also called 'hedging'). To avoid sounding bossy, speakers tend to tone down their suggestions and instructions. Here are a few strategies

You should think about this.	Oh okay, well then, **I think** this really is something that you should think about.
You should take a social sciences course.	So it **probably makes more sense** to take a social sciences course.
You should choose organizational studies.	You know, **maybe you should think about** organizational studies
You should use a corpus approach.	**Have you considered** using a corpus approach?
This should go in a separate section.	**It seems to me** that it **might make more sense** to add a separate section.

Another strategy is to stress that it's up to the other person to decide:

> It's **your decision to make**; I can't make that for you.
> Well, it **depends on** your personal interests.
> I would encourage this but **it's really up to you**.

> 📝 **Seeking confirmation**
>
> **The person receiving advice or instructions will often check with the speaker to make sure they have understood everything correctly.**
>
> > I guess that means that I get credit, **right**?
> > So it wouldn't change my grades at all, **is that what you're saying**?
> > So I should leave this turned off, **is that correct**?
> > I **just wanted to make sure** this was OK.

2.1 In these sentences, the speaker is inviting advice in a polite manner. Put the verb into the most appropriate form.

1. What .... (you / suggest)?
2. Is that what .... (you / say)?
3. I .... (think) of possibly going into genetic research.
4. What other courses .... (you / think) I should take?
5. I .... (wonder) what kind of classes I should be taking.

> 📝 Note the use of the *–ing* form in rephrasing a statement:
>
> > I'm not **saying** that this is …
> > So what I'm **claiming** is that …
> > I'm not **asking** you to …
> > Is that what you're saying?

3. Giving feedback: encouragement and criticism

- ENCOURAGING STUDENTS TO PARTICIPATE

Endorsing a response

> Okay, good. [Do not use *very well* as a response]
> Exactly!
> Spot on!
> That's a good point, actually, so let's keep that in mind.
> Yes, that makes a lot of sense.
> I'm glad you brought that up because …

Note that *fine* is usually used to reassure the other person that something is not a problem:
> I didn't mean to interrupt you.
>> No no no, that's fine.

Involving the other students

> Okay, does everybody agree with that?
> Can anyone help her out?
> You're smiling, so come on, help us out.
> Does anyone know?
> Maybe your neighbour can help?

Tactfully correcting a wrong answer

To avoid a blunt response, lecturers sometimes acknowledge that part of an answer was correct:

> Right, but there's no relationship between the two.
> Well, up to a point.
> Well, that's true. On the other hand …
> Maybe so; I mean I'm not saying that's not true but …
> Um actually, not really.
> Yeah, that's true, definitely, but how do you know …
> It could be; well, I think it does, but …

▪ FORMULATING CRITICISM

In formulating criticism, most speakers try to be tactful and constructive. These are a number of strategies that can be used.

Asking questions or reformulating points

> If you don't you choose B why not take that approach?
> So you could actually call it conditional, then?
> So essentially you are saying that …

Saying what would have been better

> Your paper would have benefitted from rereading.
> I probably wouldn't use that word.

Saying that you are not convinced

> I'm not entirely convinced.
> I would have to say that I actually am somewhat dubious on the first assumption.
> Frankly, I'm fairly sceptical about this.

To be honest, I think this is the same problem.

Saying that something is unclear or surprising

I don't see that that follows.
I'm still not so clear about the basic process.
I was surprised that you did not make the connection.
Well, actually I don't understand that answer
So, I'm a little confused.

Adding *I think* or *it seems to me*

But it seems to me that this could be classified as another category.
I think the weakest section is the last one.
That seems like a pretty central issue.

Actually

Note the frequent use of *actually* in critical comments:
    *So you could **actually** call it ... , then?*
    *Well, **actually** I don't understand ...*
    *I'm **actually** somewhat dubious about...*

UNIT IV

Dealing with practicalities

1. Classroom language

- REFERRING TO A TEXT

We're **on** p. 16.
It's **on the back** of the page (not *on the backside*)

1.	5.	2.
	6.	
	7.	
	8.	
3.	9.	4.

1. top / upper left(-hand) corner
2. top / upper right(-hand) corner
3. bottom / lower left(-hand) corner
4. bottom / lower right(-hand) corner
5. at the top of the page
6. towards the top
7. in the middle of the page
8. towards the bottom
9. at the (very) bottom

> **Page numbers**
>
> When referring to page numbers between 101 and 999, people often don't use the word *hundred*:
>
> ... at the bottom of page **four fourteen** (= p. 414)
> ... **we're on page one twenty-seven** (= p. 127)
> ... **turn to page two oh six** (= p. 206)

- DOING EXERCISES

I'd like you to **do** this **exercise** first. (not *make an exercise*, which means devising one)
If we **go through** this **exercise**, you'll see that ...
Have you already **completed** the **exercise**?

To check whether students have reached the end of an exercise:

> Are you all **done**?
> **Finished**?

Don't use *are you ready* in this context, as this means *prepared*.

> Are you **ready** to start?

- ORGANIZATIONAL DETAILS

Non-native speakers are often unfamiliar with the language used to describe the practical organization of lectures, assignments, tests, exams etc. A small range of phrases is provided below, but this is unlikely to fully cover your own situation. To find the expressions you need, pay close attention to instructions and arrangements that you come across on the websites of other universities

> We usually **take a 15 minute break** in the middle of the **class period**.
> There will be **a make-up lecture** on Friday, April 6, from 11-12 in BL 208.
> If you are unable to **attend class** (for whatever reason), please contact the instructor in advance to **notify** them of your absence.
> The **lecture notes** are **posted** online in advance of each class.
> You can arrange to **meet with** Prof Ryder to discuss your assignment.
> You need to **take the test** before meeting your advisor.
> Do not forget to **register** for the test.
> **Updates to assignments** will be **posted** on Toledo.
> Just before the exam, there will be a **review session**.

- GIVING DIRECTIONS TO ROOMS AND OFFICES

> It's **on the third floor**.
> It's **opposite** the elevators.
> The staff room is **next to** the secretary's office
> Take the second door **on the right**.
> At the main entrance, **turn left**.
> Room 91.12 is **in the basement** of the building / on the basement level.
> Room 01.130 is **at the end of the corridor**.
> Go up one **flight of stairs**.
> Walk **past** the library.
> The lecture hall is **straight ahead**.
> Take the corridor **in front of** you.

2. Infrastructure and equipment

You still have to **connect** the **power cord** to the **socket** in the wall.

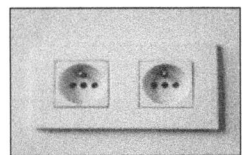

socket / wall plug

To connect, simply push **the plug** into **the socket**.
I'll just **plug in** my laptop over there.

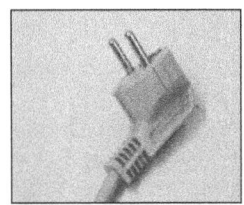

plug

Looks like we are going to need an **extension cord/extension lead**.
Don't **trip** over the cables!
Have you **connected** the cable properly?

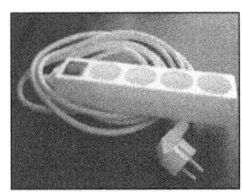

Turn/switch on the projector.
Turn/switch off the machine.
The image is blurry. Perhaps you should **adjust** the **focus**.
Why don't you **adjust the foot / feet** first?
Oops, the screen's **gone blank**!

projector

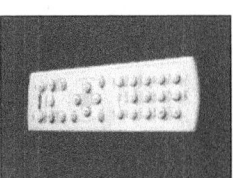

remote (control)

I still need to **switch on** the **speakers**.
Could you **turn up** the **volume**?

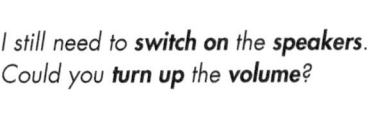

speakers

I'll first have to **plug in** the OHP. Where's the **socket**?
Press the **power button / switch**.
Tilt the mirror to move the projection up.
Try **turning the knob** to **adjust the focus**.

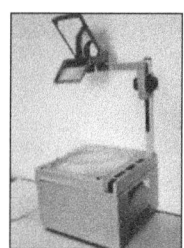

overhead projector

I'll have to **wipe** the **blackboard** first. Where's the **duster / sponge**?
Maybe you could **come to** the blackboard.
Let me first take a new **piece of chalk**.

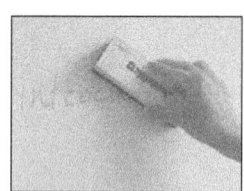

duster

Could you **switch off** the lights please?

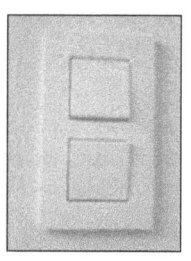

light switch

If you **pull** the cord, you can **lower / raise** the blinds.
Could you **pull down / up** the shades?
Could you please **close / draw** the curtains?

blinds / shades

Just **put** your assignment in my **pigeon hole**.
Please **drop off** your assignment at my office. You may **slide it under the door** if I'm not around.

Trying

Note the difference between *try* followed by an infinitive and *try* followed by an -ing form.

> *Try + to* (attempt to)
> **Try to set up** the room in advance.
> Please do not **try to replace** the lamp yourself.
>
> *try + ing* (see if that works)
> Have you **tried pressing** Fn and F11 simultaneously?
> Have you **tried starting** the computer with the projector plugged in?

PART THREE

Improving Spoken Language

UNIT I

Expanding vocabulary

The following pages contain exercises that will help you expand your conversational vocabulary. Do 1 or 2 exercises at a time, and note down words and expressions you would like to remember. Focus on collocations (i.e. word partnerships) rather than on single words, because this will make your language sound more natural.

1.1 **Progress and setbacks – Complete the expressions with a suitable word.**

1. Though this has **set us b**.......................... a bit, we have been working hard to compensate.
2. For the first time since I **em**.......................... **on** the project, I feel that things are gradually coming together, even though I am **slightly b**.......................... **schedule**.
3. I clearly **s**.......................... **out** with an over-ambitious agenda.
4. Anyway, I'm **back on t**.......................... now.
5. The project failed to **get off the g**..........................
6. For the social sciences, we'll have to **start from s**..........................
7. The project has been **put on h**.......................... for the time being.
8. I've **made** considerable **pr**..........................

1.2 **Complaining about lack of time – Fill the gaps.**

1. Actually, I have to **c**.......................... **up on** some work.
2. I'm .... **my eyes** in work.
3. This has **taken** .... a significant amount of my time.
4. I've been too busy. I simply haven't got **r**.......................... **to** it.
5. Most faculty are very **pressed for t**.......................... because of teaching loads.
6. We are **on a t**.......................... **schedule**, so please observe these deadlines.
7. Sorry, but I'm already **o**..........................**committed**.

1.3 Forgetfulness – Complete these sentences.

1. Let me **refresh your** ....
2. You'll have to **learn** this bit **by** ....
3. It completely **slipped my** ....
4. I've got a **memory like a** ....
5. It's on the **tip of my** ....
6. I've been **racking my** ....
7. I can't concentrate and **my mind just goes** ....
8. No, nothing **springs to** ....
9. Your name **rings a** ....

1.4 Praising seminars and presentations – Fill the gaps.

COMPREHENSIVE – REASONABLE – PROVOKING – RELEVANT – LIVELY – INSPIRING

1. The seminar was interesting and very .... **to** my work.
2. The seminar was quite .... **in scope**.
3. The **cost** of the seminar was quite ....
4. Your presentation was **thought** – .... and humorous at the same time.
5. The seminar was quite interesting as was evident from the .... **discussion**.
6. Thank you for the .... **keynote speech** you gave.

UNDERSTANDING – PROVOKED – BLEND – COVERED – ARGUED – EYE-OPENER

1. It was **an interesting** .... of history and modern technology
2. **Several topics** were ....
3. The speaker demonstrated **a thorough** .... of the topic.
4. The seminar was quite well attended, ... **much discussion**, and was appreciated by all
5. Most of the participants felt that the seminar was **quite an** ....
6. The presentation was **well** – .... and well illustrated

> ### Useful evaluative adjectives
>
> quite fascinating – balanced – informative – impressive – easy to follow – well-prepared – relevant – enlightening – inspiring – informative – comprehensive – stimulating – thorough – challenging – effective – though-provoking – well-argued – outstanding
>
> rather technical – boring – sketchy – obscure – irrelevant – confusing – bland – superficial – sloppy

▶ Expanding vocabulary

1.5 **Criticizing** – Complete the sentence with a suitable word.

PAR – SIGHTED – CRACKED – DESIRED – OBSCURE – EFFECTIVE

1. Technical training may not be **all it's** .... **up to be**.
2. However, the practical application of their research **leaves a lot to be** ....
3. In consequence, there is a bottom line, even when the content of a paper is acceptable, if the quality of the English is **below** ....
4. That's a very **short-**.................... **view**. In the long term, it would be better to ...
5. Unfortunately, the seminar was **not as** .... as it could have been.
6. I felt the **topic** was rather ....

1.6 **Add a suitable verb.**

1. To .... matters worse, ...
2. To .... it mildly, ...
3. To .... a long story short, ...
4. To .... it in a nutshell, ...
5. To .... the ball rolling, ...
6. To .... that another way, ...

1.7 **What is the missing word in all these expressions?**

1. We must **keep an open** ....
2. The thought never **crossed** my ....
3. Thanks, I'll **bear it in** ....
4. I **changed** my ....
5. I can't **make up** my ....

1.8 **Communication problems** – Complete the gaps.

1. He's **missing the p**....................
2. We're **going r**.................... **in circles**.
3. We're obviously not **on the same wavel**....................
4. I'm afraid **you've l**.................... **me**. Could you explain that again?
5. I gave some thought on how to **get my message ac**.................... effectively.
6. The audience was very attentive, but not very **respo**....................

1.9 *Detail* or *details*? Encircle the best option.

1. I'd better fill you in on the **detail / details.**

2. I'll also **go into some detail / details** about the components involved in the system.
3. To be sure, things are not so simple when we **get down to the detail / details**.
4. I'll just guide you through the **detail / details**.
5. Several examples were discussed **in greater detail / details**.

1.10 **Complete the gaps with a suitable past participle: one will have to be used twice.**

SERVED – SAID – GRANTED – SIDETRACKED – DESIRED

1. Places will be allocated on a first come, first ……………… basis.
2. Don't take anything for ………………
3. That's easier ……………… than done.
4. It leaves a lot to be ………………
5. He keeps getting ………………
6. That ……………… , I do believe ISPs should take some basic best practice steps toward securing their own networks.

1.11 **Q & A – Insert the correct preposition or adverb.**

1. I'll get straight …………… **the point**.
2. I'm afraid I can't answer this one …………… **the top of my head**.
3. Would you care to **elaborate** …………… that, John?
4. Okay, I have to admit I'm not entirely sure what you're asking. So please **bear** …………… **me**.
5. Now, …………… **I said earlier**, I may have misunderstood the point you were making.
6. What exactly were you **getting** ……………?
7. Obviously, there's so **much more** …………… **this** dissertation than what I'm talking about here.

1.12 **Add the missing nouns to these verb / noun collocations.**

1. I'm sure there's a much easier way to **tackle this p**………………
2. We shouldn't **lose s**………………of the need for legal parameters.
3. These advances have **paved the w**………………for important new developments.
4. Obviously, his comments **carry a lot of w**………………
5. We shouldn't **jump to c**………………
6. Our aim is to **bridge the g**………………between theory and practice.

7. That seems to **make s**.........................
8. We cannot **overlook the f**..........................that this was a very small sample.
9. I think your observation is correct, but you're **drawing the wrong c**..........................
 from it.
10. This view is **gaining g**..........................

1.13 **Insert an appropriate adjective.**

PLAIN – DUE – FOREGONE – BROAD – USEFUL

1. In general, this approach is presented as **a** .... **conclusion**.
2. The results will be published **in** .... **course**.
3. If you can come up with a workable definition, then it should be more or less .... **sailing**.
4. Obviously, we asked a much .... **range** of questions than that.
5. Unfortunately it did not **prove** very ....

OVERWHELMING – VALID – CONSISTENT – SKETCHY – NARROW

6. The information is **far too** .... to be of any use.
7. Our study was more .... **in scope**.
8. That's still a .... **point**.
9. There is .... **evidence** that this was indeed the case.
10. Our results are .... **with** that hypothesis.

1.14 **Complete the phrasal verbs.**

1. Simply use the interactive search facility to **narrow** .... the options.
2. Perhaps I can **pass** these ....
3. Please remember to **switch** .... the projector after your presentation.
4. I just need somewhere to **plug** .... my laptop.
5. Unfortunately, the seminar was a failure as only few people **turned** ....
6. What this **boils** .... to is that this influence is pretty much random.
7. This **ties** .... with research we have done, which shows that …
8. I wouldn't **rule** .... the possibility.
9. We must **weigh** .... the options carefully before we take a decision.
10. The basic message I'm trying to **get** .... here is quite simple.
11. It basically **comes** .... to this.

1.15 Add the correct prepositions.

1. Can I just very quickly **pick up** .... a point you made before?
2. We'll **come back** .... that later if we can.
3. That plays an important role .... **this stage**.
4. Could you bring us **up to date** .... the latest developments?
5. That is the **key** .... analysing such data.
6. .... **my knowledge**, nothing has been written about this relationship.

1.16 Referring to other research – Complete the gaps.

1. He **came** .... **with** a number of interesting suggestions.
2. If we take this view as valid, then we have to **take on** .... more recent findings.
3. **By and** ...., most studies show that there is indeed an effect.
4. If you want more information about recent work and the **st**............ **of the field,** take a look at the reference list.

1.17 Describing relationships – Complete the gaps.

1. These factors **go hand in** ....
2. Such decisions **tie** .... **closely with** other research projects.
3. They **relate** .... **each other** in a non-hierarchical way.
4. These water systems are **interr**................
5. Ethanol abuse is **strongly as**............... with hypothermia.
6. They are **inextricably l**............... by an energy flow.
7. Social relationships are **intertw**............... with the physical environment.
8. These two are seen as **inti**............... **connected**.
9. These have way too often been **lu**............... **together** into very broad categories.

UNIT II

Avoiding common errors

1. Vocabulary

1.1 Verbs like *say, tell, explain* and *discuss* are often misused. Can you correct the following?

1. What I would like to do is present you my research > ....
2. Let me first explain you what the research questions are > ....
3. I'll tell a bit about methodology first > ....
4. As I told earlier > ....
5. I will give some remarks about > ....
6. I would just like to tell that you can interrupt me > ....
7. We're discussing about the causes now > ....

> **Usage rules**
> - *tell*:
> - *say*:
> - *explain*:
> - *discuss*:

1.2 Sometimes two similar words or phrases get mixed up. Can you correct the following?

1. In contrary > ....
2. Regarding to the first aspect > ....
3. My doctoral research considers a subject that...> ....
4. ... at least what the climate considers > ....
5. I have a couple of critics > ....

6. Aside from these colonists > ....
7. It's still in a very initial status > ....
8. You are mistaking if you think that ...> ....
9. Can you deduct the implications? > ....
10. I'll shortly describe the new design. > ....
11. I'll discuss social and economical problems > ....
12. The participants might think we're trying to control them. > ....
13. At last, I would like to present two case studies > ....

1.3 **Add the correct preposition.**

1. How did they **react** .... that information.
2. I will give some **characteristics** .... this strategy.
3. We decided to **focus** .... an interest group.
4. The consumer is clearly **satisfied** .... these brands.
5. When you want to **go** .... a conference ...
6. Belgian law should **apply** .... these cases.
7. The **answers** .... your questions are ...
8. This happened only .... some **occasions**.

1.4 **Add a preposition if one is necessary.**

1. When we **look** .... internal communication ...
2. Ontology is not **concerned** .... these matters.
3. I will **come back** .... that later on.
4. I will **ask** .... the person in the other department if ...
5. Some layers claim they are .... **a disadvantage**.
6. It's a restriction you keep .... **mind** when you do research.
7. They believe that, ... **the long term**, they will earn more.
8. We'll **discuss** .... in our next class.

1.5 **Correct the mistakes.**

1. This is a *classical* example > ....
2. Participants were asked to give *critique* on a product > ....
3. I will now *shortly* describe our work > ....
4. Every 30 minutes, I will *come in between* to guide you ....
5. This is *facultative literature* > ....
6. It slowly *evoluated* in this direction > ....

> Non-native speakers often overuse *a little bit*. Below are a few alternatives:
>
> This is a **somewhat** controversial area.
> I have **a bit of a** problem.
> I'm using a **slightly** different model.
> This is a **little** more common.
> It's a **fairly** small department.
> Let me tell you **something** about the data first.
> Let me give you just a **brief** overview.

2. Grammar

The following pages contain an overview of some of the most common grammar errors in presentations by non-native speakers, particularly speakers of Dutch.

- ADJECTIVES AND ADVERBS

2.1 **Speakers of Dutch frequently mix up adjectives and adverbs. In the sentences below, underline the correct option.**

1. This is a *wide / widely* accepted definition.
2. It's of course a *typical / typically* Belgian problem.
3. We have debates on other things than *pure / purely* technical matters.
4. Their education programme is *good / well* established, which is perhaps *not surprising / surprisingly*.
5. I thought the presentation was very *good / well* structured.
6. You covered this topic very *brief / briefly*.
7. I found it *easy / easily* to follow.
8. They *voluntary / voluntarily* chose to do this.
9. I'll be very *brief / briefly* on this.
10. I will focus on managers, and *more specific / specifically*, global managers.
11. It is *free / freely* downloadable.
12. This is just a number that it *automatic / automatically* generates.
13. Let's first see how *quick / quickly* we can proceed with this part.
14. This is *typical / typically* of the formalist movement.
15. People actually do this *unconscious / unconsciously*.

2.2 Insert the adverbial in the correct position.

1. Are you only looking at causes?	THEN
2. A script file has the extension .exp.	ALWAYS
3. I started my post-doctoral fellowship.	THIS YEAR
4. I would insert an article.	THERE
5. I had the impression that you were hesitating.	SOMETIMES
6. Most of the literature is in English.	AS WELL
7. You should focus on the immediate effects.	MORE
8. You can see two reactions.	HERE

Insert *now* in the correct position.
1. You can go to Toledo.
2. They take a stricter approach.
3. This matrix has two rows and four columns.

Insert *already* in the correct position.
1. You can conduct some analysis on a newspaper article.
2. Of course we've omitted the details here.
3. The logo exists in Spain.
4. The word itself says what its characteristics are.

Insert *also* in the correct position.
1. We do that quite often.
2. We have to be aware that …
3. In this way, you obtain a chi-square value.
4. In order to understand, you have to look at …

- ARTICLES

2.3 The use of articles in English is tricky, especially for speakers of languages that do not have a similar article system. Insert *the* or *a* where necessary.

1. The predicted interaction was found in ……….. both studies
2. She is ……….. member of ….
3. In ……….. Roman imperial times …
4. This work is ……….. classic.
5. It is ……….. different subdivision.
6. It's ……….. good advice to read through the course material before you come to class.
7. He's ……….. philosopher.
8. The increase was revealed by ……….. multivariate analysis.

9. These studies have opened recent discussions concerning .... nature of .... rationality.
10. The format was a multiple-choice design with .... most questions having four or five choices.

> **Usage rules for articles**
>
> - An **indefinite article** (*a / an*) is used when the noun is unspecified and singular.
>
>   > She has recently published **a study** on ....
>
> - A **definite article** (*the*) is used to refer to one or more identified things or persons
>
>   > **The study** raises questions about whether ...
>
> - **No article** is used when the noun is unspecified and plural
>
>   > She has published **articles** in a variety of **journals.**
>
> - **No article** is used with unspecified uncountable nouns
>
>   > He has also conducted **research** on migration.
>
> - Note that some nouns have both countable and uncountable (more abstract) uses.
>
>   > In my talk, I will present **an analysis** of quasi-particle wave functions.
>   > We undertook systematic **analysis** of post-operative pain scores.

- CONDITIONALS

2.4 Put the verb between brackets in the appropriate form.

1. If this country .... (*become*) a member, there will be a lot of problems.
2. It would have been clearer if you .... (*use*) more examples.
3. If supermarkets .... (*offer*) more organic products, consumers would automatically buy more.
4. If I .... (*have*) to choose, I would take the second part.
5. If they had been attacked, they .... (*report*) it.
6. The lecturer suggested I contact you to see if you .... (*schedule*) an extra tutorial.

2.5 In the sentences below, choose between *if* and *when*.

1. I'm allowed to use this material *if / when* I acknowledge them in the Foreword.
2. *If / When* you were to believe that, you would be irrational.
3. I'll check up on this *if / when* I get back to the office.
4. Maybe you can finish that *if / when* class is over.
5. Well, I'd be really surprised *if / when* this really helped reduce crime rates.

Usage rules for conditionals

- Do not mix up *if* and *when*

    > When I go to the conference …. (= I'm sure I will go)
    > If I go to the conference …. (= perhaps I will go)
    > When / If I go to a conferenc e …. (= whenever)

- Do not use *will* or *would* in if-clauses

    > * If they would ask the authorities, …. > If they asked / were to ask the authorities
    > * If you would have been there, … > If you had been there …

- Note that *will* / *would* can be used after *if* provided that the meaning is *be willing to*

    > If you'd like to come this way, please
    > If you'll just fill in this form, please
    > If only he would listen to me

- Note the use of *if* in fixed expressions

    > if in doubt – if not – if possible – if necessary – if anything – if only – if ever – if at all – if so

■ COUNTABLE AND UNCOUNTABLE NOUNS

2.6 Circle the correct answer.

1. There are so *much – many* pieces.
2. We found *little – few* evidence that the program had any effect on them.
3. I had *much – many* setbacks along the way.
4. Actually, quite an *amount – a number* of students has asked me the same question.
5. They will try to put as *much – many* new products on the market as possible.
6. Let's talk about *a little – a few* of these examples.

7. So there are *much – many* more linkages.
8. Most pay *little – few* attention to how those animals were raised.
9. Did they invest *much – many* time in it?
10. A large *amount – number* of problems.

> **Usage rules for many / much – few / little – fewer / less – number / amount**
>
> | COUNTABLE | UNCOUNTABLE |
> | --- | --- |
> | many | much |
> | number | amount |
> | fewer | less |
> | few / a few | little / a little |

■ PRONOUNS

2.7 Choose the correct relative pronouns – sometimes the 2 options are possible.

1. And this is a brand *who / that* is actually better than others.
2. It's one of the schools *who / which* teach Cornish.
3. That's the part *that / where* I'm currently working on.
4. A student *which / who* participated in the study.
5. Are these the people *that / who* voted for Bush?
6. This is the kind of project *that / which* no committee would have accepted.
7. The project failed to get off the ground, *what / which* was of course unfortunate.
8. For example, the Hawaiian Islands, *that / which* are entirely of volcanic origin, have formed in the middle of the Pacific Ocean.
9. I'll pay particular attention to the debate *that / which* surrounded his ideas.
10. The man *who / that* invented the algorithm was a librarian in the Vatican library.

Usage rules for relative pronouns

- *who* refers only to people; *which* refers only to things; *that* can refer to both people and things.
- in restrictive relative clauses (which help to identify the antecedent), use *that* or *which* to refer to things. In informal style, an object pronoun can even be omitted.

    The party that she voted for .... / The party which she voted for ... / The party she voted for.

- in non-restrictive relative clauses (which offer additional information – between commas) use *which* to refer to things

    The CDU, which is leading in opinion polls, would prefer to ...

- To refer to a whole clause, use *which* (not *what*)

    Standards are improving, which is perhaps not surprising.

	People	Things
Subject	who that (restrictive only)	which that (restrictive only)
Object	who / whom that (restrictive only)	which that (restrictive only)
Possessive	whose	whose / of which

2.8 **Personal and reflexive pronouns: correct the mistake in every sentence.**

1. These factors have manifested theirselves through significant eutrophication problems ...
2. If you look closely at the cells itself, you will notice ...
3. He still has to learn to think for hisself.
4. You can take another computer, but you still need to switch him on.
5. Maybe we can do this ourself?

■ VERB FORMS AND TENSES

2.9 Rephrase, paying particular attention to the verb forms.

1. We need to take into account the buildings that were existing > ....
2. I'm only working on this for 2 months > ....
3. It's existing for two years > ....
4. This study is dealing with Neo-platonism > ....
5. She has already been in Leuven for 2 years before I arrived > ....
6. I am living in Leuven for 3 years > ....
7. Since then, she works in the History department > ....
8. This here is representing an amount of biomass > ....
9. From here on, Chapter two is starting > ....
10. I teach this course for 4 years > ....

> **Tenses: a few rules of thumb**
>
> - Use the **past tense** to refer to a definite time in the (distant or recent) past ("*then*") – use the **present perfect** to refer to an event or activity that is seen as continuing *up to now*
>
>   *I saw him last week*
>   *I've been working on this for a month*
>
> - Use **continuous** forms to express limited duration
>
>   *I'm living in Leuven (temporarily)*
>   *Shares are falling (later they will rise again)*
>   *He was just leaving when I came in (he was in the process of leaving)*
>   *I have been studying French (seen as incomplete)*

2.10 The following sentences all contain a common error. Identify the mistake.

1. And the last point why I'm not agree with > ....
2. They are used to buy books over the Internet > ....
3. Customers that are already switched > ....
4. What exactly means law? > ....
5. I don't mind to answer these questions > ....
6. I agree with most things that are already said > ....
7. I give you 5 minutes for that > ....
8. Ok, I start with a definition of the main concepts > ....

- DUTCHISMS

2.11 **Speakers of Dutch tend to combine singular pronouns with plural verb forms in direct translation of Dutch (*Het / dat zijn ...*).**

1. Are it only the specialists in the field who can judge that? > ....
2. That are efficient markets > ....
3. That are the brands that are owned by the retailer > ....
4. As you can see here, it were ... > ....
5. But this are details > ....
6. We call this elongated stone pieces > ....
7. So that are the types of information sources that we use > ....
8. It are the genes that have evolved due to selective pressure > ....

2.12 **The following phrases sound like translated Dutch – Rephrase.**

1. Yes, but there exist however some anomalies > ....
2. And there was said that ...> ....
3. Can there anything be done? > ....
4. I focused on poverty and his effect on children > ....
5. To be honest, that's not my topic of Ph.D > ....
6. Last year, I did a research on > ....
7. a little bit of information > ....
8. Yes, but not in all of Belgium > ....
9. people who are member of the party > ....
10. A colleague of us said that ... > ....
11. How is it called? > ....
12. We wanted that there was a distinction between Church and State > ....
13. Or it is man-made, or it is there already > ....
14. This is a model of how wires on a chip look like > ....
15. There have been made modern editions > ....

> While the language of presentations and lectures is less formal than the language of academic writing, it may be better to avoid certain colloquialisms.
>
> *Diversification was **kind of** a hot topic.*
> *The definition I'm **gonna** make.*
> *It was, **like**, frustrating, **you know**.*

UNIT III

Improving pronunciation

All the exercises in this unit are accompanied by a sound file. To access this file, go to the Acco website (www.uitgeverijacco.be/academicspokenenglish) and choose "downloads" in the menu on the left. Then enter the code ay86n2 and follow the instructions.

1. Word stress

If you stress the wrong syllable in a word, this will make it much harder for the audience to understand what you are saying. If you are unsure about word stress, consult a dictionary, such as the Macmillan Dictionary (http://www.macmillandictionary.com), which offers phonetic transcriptions and has an audio function. Another excellent resource is http://www.howjsay.com/, a pronunciation dictionary with instant sound, which also contains a wide range of technical terms. If the term you are looking for is not included, try the following strategy: type the term into Google and add the search term *pronunciation*. For instance, a search for *borrelia burgdorferi + pronunciation* yields a number of useful pages, including a *Lyme Disease Pronunciation Guide*, where you can simply click on the words to hear the correct pronunciation.

The exercises in this unit focus on the most common academic vocabulary.

1.1 Read out these sentences – Add problem words to the grid below.

Set I

1. The categories they used in their analysis seem somewhat arbitrary.
2. Moving on to the content of my project, there are three key areas that I would like to highlight this morning.
3. There are a number of discrepancies in the framework he developed.
4. At least three distinct ideas have contributed to the development of the doctrine that legislative power cannot be delegated. [*Note that 'idea" has 3 syllables – it should not be pronounced as ID*]

5. Well, look at it this way: mathematics and physics are actually complementary subjects.
6. Although the results of their studies are not directly applicable, their methods form a basis for possible further investigation.
7. My colleague sits on the committee, so it's a bit of an awkward situation.
8. He conducted a study into the effects of light on children of elementary school age.
9. It's an innovative approach, guaranteed to generate controversy among the employees.
10. Deliberate ambiguity can contribute to the effectiveness and richness of a work.

Set II

1. In order to test the null hypothesis, we need to determine to what extent the observed frequencies diverge from the expected frequencies.
2. It's hard to differentiate between the categories.
3. This is not consistent with a multi-disciplinary approach.
4. Contrary to our expectations, we found this sample of men to be relatively well-educated
5. There are many industrial plants that discharge heavy metals, and those heavy metals in particular cause a lot of environmental damage here.
6. The speaker discussed some of the psychological effects associated with the increasing capabilities of new technology [*The "p" in "psychological" is a silent p – it should not be pronounced*].
7. The preliminary results need to be interpreted with caution.
8. If Galileo hadn't lived in a Christian society, perhaps the study of astronomy and geophysics would have progressed at a much faster rate.
9. On the other hand, we may need to reconsider our current grading practices.
10. She also provides administrative support to the International Office.

Set III

1. Clear and convincing evidence is sometimes characterized as 75% certainty.
2. They commented that the general approach was very reasonable and appropriate given the inadequacies of available data.
3. Other chapters elaborate on the specific effects of the policy.
4. Our primary objective is to investigate the techniques used for measuring the costs and benefits associated with implementing computer systems.
5. She coordinated the campaign with great skill and enthusiasm.
6. The questionnaire was distributed to around 1000 respondents.

7. Accuracy here is comparable to information content in a single cell response.
8. The control group reported a higher preparation level, but no other significant differences occurred.
9. What is the statistical significance of these results?
10. Adult learners perform best when they are able to negotiate aspects of their learning.

Set IV

1. Unfortunately, my colleague and I differ in one respect.
2. I would be interested in hearing your views on these dramatic results.
3. Will these techniques be equally productive?
4. That conclusion seems hardly justifiable, so I remain sceptical.
5. Is there a connection between aesthetic development and cognitive development?
6. This analysis attempts to extrapolate the percentage of patients with appropriate care from Table 1.
7. It's a comparative historical analysis of psychotherapy.
8. The increase can be attributed to the formation of the inter-metallic compounds.
9. This appears to confirm our initial diagnosis.
10. Well, what is particularly interesting about the market is 65 percent of these women wear size 14 or greater.

Set V

1. Americans appear to be ambivalent about what role the government should play in regulating the dietary supplement industry.
2. Converging technologies provide a direct means of communicating interdisciplinary research.
3. Figure 1 shows the relationships among the components of the inventory.
4. The results of some experimental studies show that students of all abilities benefit from participating in a heterogeneous cooperative group.
5. The Engineering curriculum places a strong emphasis on the Student Selected Component in Year 4.
6. Accreditation of Prior Achievement (APA) is a process that enables people to gain recognition and accreditation for what they already know,
7. Multiple representations may complement each other with regard to their content.
8. An appendix describes the use of software for constructing questionnaires and processing response data.
9. The only legitimate conclusion is that this theory is invalid.
10. The mesh is rolled either along the diagonal axis or along the other two axes.

1.2 In identical verb-noun pairs, there is often a stress difference:

to de**crease**: stress on the 2nd syllable
a **de**crease: stress on the 1st syllable

1. We've all made a lot of *progress* the last few weeks.
   We've *progressed* quite a lot on this particular subject.
2. This shows you a detailed *record* of what happened.
   First *record* the initial value.
3. There's a huge *increase* as N goes up.
   As you can see it *increases* dramatically.
4. And this was the origin of all *conflict*.
   Interestingly, some of these criteria may *conflict*.
5. The Flemish credit system is based on the European Credit *Transfer* System.
   You can *transfer* your grade to next year.
6. Here's my email *address*.
   I'd like to *address* both these issues today.
7. They examined the *attributes* of a happy and successful life for adolescents
   These changes can be *attributed* to many factors.
8. Who can put a date on this *object*?
   Some *objected* to this very strongly.
9. They're based on a fairly large *survey* we did last summer.
   She used an online program to *survey* parents about their smoking behaviour.
10. After the break, he's going to *update* us on this topic.
    These data are from 2002, so they're in need of an *update*.

1.3 In some cases, there is no such stress shift:

1. Do you have *access* to the P-drive?
   You can *access* these exercises via our website.
2. This is just a quick *review* of what we've already talked about.
   I'd like you to *review* this before our next class.
3. And then I'll talk about our ongoing *research*. *(both the 1st and the 2nd syllable can be stressed)*
   That's why I wanted to *research* this subject. *(both the 1st and the 2nd syllable can be stressed)*
4. You can't prove cause and *effect* here.
   You need this to *effect* a change in policy.

1.4 The following sentences contain problem words:

1. Don't forget you have an *exam* on Tuesday!
2. Do you have any additional *comments*?
3. There's been a lot of *debate* over this.
4. Use *parentheses* to enclose search terms.
5. They've just released a new *report*.
6. How would you *interpret* this?
7. They *differ* in a number of important ways.
8. It's basically just a *series* of anecdotes.
9. This is a *serious* problem.
10. These are the *variables* that are affecting the *development*.

Add words that you mispronounce to this grid. Review regularly.

STRESS 1ST SYLLABLE	STRESS 2ND SYLLABLE	STRESS 3RD SYLLABLE
		STRESS 4TH SYLLABLE

2. Consonants

- VOICED FINAL CONSONANTS

Don't forget to lengthen the vowel if it is followed by a voiced consonant. There is a difference between:

> bat and bad
> cap and cab
> back and bag
> rice and rise
> safe and save

2.1 BAT / BAD – Practise the difference.

at / add	hat / had
bat / bad	lift / lived
coat / code	set / said
foot / food	sight / side

2.2 CAP / CAPS – Practise the difference.

cap / cab	rip / rib
crap / crab	rope / robe
cup / cub	ripe / tribe

2.3 BACK / BAG – Practise the difference.

dock / dog	leak / league
back / bag	lock / log
pick / pig	ankle / angle

2.4 RICE / RISE – Practise the difference.

advice / advise	loose / lose
east / eased	price / prize
fierce / fears	race / raise
rice / rise	this / these

In the following words [s] is pronounced as [z]:

> easier – easy – reason – present – presentation – physical – socializing – observed – using

This is not the case in the following words:

> analysis – dissertation – research – hypothesis

2.5 SAFE / SAVE – Practise the difference.

a life / alive	leaf / leave
belief / believe	proof / prove
lift / lived	safe / save

- ENGLISH [TH]

When pronouncing [th], there should be a clear difference with [t] and [d]. On the other hand, [th] shouldn't sound like an [s] or a [z] or an [f] either.

2.6 Practise the difference between [th] and [t].

tin – thin	team – theme
tank – thank	fort – forth
tree – three	part – path

2.7 Practise the difference between [th] and [d].

dare – there	breed – breathe
Dan – than	wordy – worthy
dough – though	dead – death

2.8 Practise the difference between [th] and [s].

sink / think	pass / path
seem / theme	tense / tenth
sum / thumb	sought / thought
sing / thing	worse / worth

2.9 Read the sentences below.

1. I think there's something wrong with me.
2. My throat has been sore for three days. And I'm thirsty.
3. I'm thinking of going to the Health Centre.
4. I don't think it's worth it.
5. You forgot Theo's birthday on Thursday.
6. As a theologian, I'm interested in the concept of the Virgin Birth.

- ENGLISH [V]

If you are told that you tend to pronounce [v] as [w], try to give the sound more friction.

2.10 **Practise the following words.**

advantages – advocated – available – avoid – develop – development – diverse – even – have – however – individuals – innovate – invited – involved – levels – moreover – over – positive – previous – provided – relevant – revealed – Soviet – valid – value – variables

- ENGLISH [W]

English [w] is more rounded than Dutch [w] – for instance, to pronounce *when* say something like *oe-wen*.

2.11 **Practise the [w] sound.**

1. I would like to make one remark.
2. Where are the women?
3. Why would he leave his wife?
4. When is the wedding?
5. I was wondering why you would want to do this.

- WORD-FINAL [NG]

Some speakers pronounce [ng] as [nk]. When pronouncing words with [ng] take care not to add a [k] sound.

2.12 **Practise the following words.**

agreeing – bring – depending – following – linger – living – longer – morning – right-wing – sing-song – asking

- ENGLISH [H]

Some speakers have a guttural [h]. For instance, they tend to pronounce the [h] in *have* like the [j] in Spanish *Javier*.

2.13 **Practise the following words.**

behave – behaviour – have – health care – how did this happen – human – a hundred – him – hardware – heaven and hell

- SOFT AND HARD [G]

The [g] in English can be pronounced soft, as in *general*, or hard, as in *go*.

2.14 Practise the following words with soft [g].

budget – huge – intelligence – legislation – pedagogical – strategy – logical – psychology

3. Vowels

For the sake of convenience, in the headings below the vowels sounds are represented by words they occur in.

- PART & PORT

3.1 Practise the difference.

port / part	corn / car
or / are	store / star
pork / park	

3.2 Read the sentences below.

1. Let's park the car here. It's not far.
2. He is a member of the Labour party.
3. To give you just one example ….
4. I'll try to stay calm.
5. When did you join the Arts department?

- NO & NOW

3.3 Practise the difference.

know / now	or / our
a low / allow	soul / sour
	row (in a table) / row (quarrel)

3.4 Read the sentences below.

1. Don't shout so loud.
2. How much does it cost? It's worth about a thousand pounds.
3. I had a terrible row with my supervisor.
4. This is shown in the lower row of Figure 3.
5. When in doubt, leave it out.
6. And now I'll start the Powerpoint presentation.
7. We should not lower our standards, though.

- NO & NOT

3.5 Practise the following words, taking care not to lengthen the [o] sound.

project – knowledge – discover – problems – topic – product

- BED & BAD

3.6 Practise the difference.

head / had	met / mat
beg / bag	peck / pack
lend / land	pet / pat
Ken / can	kettle / cattle
pen / pan	then / than

3.7 Practise the following phrases, taking care not to pronounce [a] as [e].

1. These are very drastic measures.
2. It's a gradual process.
3. As a matter of fact, that's not valid.
4. Actually, this solution is not satisfactory.

3.8 Practise the following phrases, taking care not to pronounce [e] as [a].

1. Well, in this sense
2. I'm feeling much better now
3. That doesn't seem very relevant.
4. I have a number of questions.
5. It's a very high level.
6. She made a very good impression.

- BED & BID

3.9 Practise the difference.

bed / bid	head / hit
dead / did	led / lit
ten / tin	vector / Victor

3.10 Practise the following phrases.

1. in the mid-seventies
2. the main influence
3. I cannot predict that this will happen
4. to make a good impression

- LIVE & LEAVE

3.11 Practise the difference between short and long [i].

live / leave	did / deed
this / these	rid / read
still / steal	rich / reach
filling / feeling	

3.12 Practise the short [i] sound in the following words.

activity – big – continue – criminals – familiar – give – individual – issue – limits – a little bit – mirror – physical – political – prison – pyramid – rich – ritual – shifts – split – still – this

3.13 Practise the long [i] sound in the following phrases.

please leave me alone – these procedures – are these yours? – try to reach your goals – I'll give you the sheet – here's some feedback – this is the reason – these machines – feelings

- CUT

3.14 Some speakers pronounce *cut* as *caht*. Practise this sound in the following words.

cut – current – studies – such – young – youngsters – function – funds – but

- EDUCATION

3.15 Practise the following words, paying attention to the [u] sound: for instance, say *pop–you–lation* rather than *poppelation*.

population – education – – individual – regular – particularly – situation – occupy

- THE + VOWEL

If the article *the* is followed by a word starting with a vowel, the two words should be linked up.

3.16 Practise the following phrases

the administrative system – the annual report – the auditor – the impact – the only offer

Key to the Exercises

Part One

1. Features of spoken language

Exercise 1.2

The following sentences are easier to process than the original version.
1. In this research project we aim to develop new methods and to apply mathematical simulations to real world engineering problems. These problems are situated in three principal areas: ...
2. So, far right ideologies have been the focus of renewed academic interest. And since the European recent election, political interest has increased as well.
3. It's commonly assumed that obesity and TV viewing are directly related, but new research new research into the effects of sedentary behaviour has challenged this assumption.
4. In the next section, I will examine some of the basic principle of Young's argument and then I will compare these with existing textbook interpretations. What I would like to do is show that these existing interpretations are extremely reductive for two reasons. First, they ignore Young's interest in non-empirical condition. And second, they fail to take into account Young's criticism of the traditional understanding of the transcendental.
5. If you want to improve the quality of information for patients, you need to consider the media that are used, but you should also look the quality of the content. And that's an area that is still very much neglected..
6. So this study suggests that there is a causal relationship between employee satisfaction and increased productivity but that assumption can be questioned because it might lead to overestimates as well as to underestimates of the competitiveness effect.
7. Although depression occurs very frequently in this population, it remains one of the most underdiagnosed disorders and as a result it is often left untreated. Yet it may have harmful effects on cellular immunity, including those aspects of the immune system that are affected by HIV.

Exercise 2.2

1. Are you with me?
2. pick up / left off
3. come up with
4. without saying
5. in due course
6. leave it at that
7. pick up
8. touched on
9. wraps up

Exercise 2.3

1. on – 2. going – 3. down – 4.to – 5.hang
1. started – 2. down – 3. back – 4. across – 5. into

2. Structure

Exercise 1.1   18

In this presentation / lecture I'd like to   19

1. talk to you
2. tell you about
3. introduce you to
4. take a look at
5. report on the results
6. explore the issue

I'll start by   19

1. filling you in on
2. making a few remarks
3. bringing you up-to-date
4. describing
5. giving you an overview of
6. looking at

… and then I'll go on to   19

1. take you through
2. discuss the implications (highlight also possible)
3. make recommendations
4. put … into perspective
5. highlight key features (discuss also possible)
6. examine how

Exercise 2.3   24

Typical of conversational style: anyhow – by the way – let me recap – what's more – OK so – right – well – so then – actually – the thing is – and besides

Exercise 2.4   24

1. going / covered
2. any
3. due
4. on / briefly
5. turn
6. brings
7. moving
8. draw
9. at
10. put

Exercise 2.5

1. elaborate
2. mention
3. comes / boils
4. back
5. as
6. just
7. clear
8. points
9. wraps
10. shed
11. leave
12. take

Exercise 3.1

1. What I'd like to do is move on to the question of ...
2. What I'm going to do is describe briefly the main ....
3. What I've tried to do is put our recent difficulties ....
4. What I'll be doing is making a case for ...
5. So, what I'm saying is ...
6. What I'd like you to do is ask yourself ....
7. What I'm going to be doing is looking at ...
8. So, what I've done is put together ...
9. What you might do is try to find a synonym.

3. Visuals

Exercise 1.1

vertical axis
horizontal dotted lines
the solid black line
light grey shaded area

Exercise 1.2

1. diverge
2. crosses
3. determine
4. selected
5. plotted

1. hits
2. decline
3. flattens out
4. move
5. fit

Exercise 1.3 32
1. distributed evenly **along** the Y-axis.
2. cross each other **at** this point.
3. a sharp drop **in** maximum wave-height.
4. look **at** the top panel.
5. X is less than or equal **to** Z
6. Divide both sides **by** point-eight then
7. subtract one equation **from** the other?
8. Multiply that **by** the square root of one

Exercise 2.1 33
1. **Nearly** half of this population suffers from symptoms of burnout.
2. The bar for 2001 reaches to **just under** 40% .
3. And you'll see here that, as you go up in the basin, that the elevation increases from **approximately** nine hundred meters to **almost** two thousand meters
4. The chart on my next slide shows that **just over** half of all respondents reported that ....
5. **Roughly speaking, about** fifty percent of all lupus patients will develop this nephritis.
6. The graph climbs from **roughly** 10 percent to 25 percent between 2000 and 2008.
7. But after all, the sun makes up **some** 99 percent of the solar system.

4. **Delivery**

Exercise 3.1 39
The aim of the workshop is threefold:
- to showcase our research
- to provide an overview of ongoing projects
- to examine the role of external partners

PART TWO

1. Handling the question-and-answer session

Exercise 1.1 44

1. You didn't, **I believe**, talk about the... I didn't hear that anyway.
2. I was wondering if ...
3. Yes, I was **just** going to ask you if...
4. **Just** something to share,...
5. I'm curious ... ?
6. Yes, I **just** wondered about ...
7. I've got a question. I'd like to know how ...

Exercise 1.2 44

1. I don't **quite** understand ... ('I just don't understand' would sound very direct)
2. Could I **just** ask you on ... / We are not **quite** clear which ...
3. I'd **just** like to point out that ...
4. Could I **just** make a point about ...
5. I'm afraid I'm not **quite** clear what ...
6. **Just** remind me ...
7. Can I **just** say ...
8. I'm sorry but I don't **quite** get your point.
9. **Just** one thing worries me ....
10. Sorry, but I don't **quite** see ... / Could you **just** explain ...

Exercise 1.4 47

1. When you were **dealing with** lexicographical typologies, you **commented on** the complex task of matching dictionaries to the typological scheme. Could you **elaborate on** that?
2. When you were **talking about** Raymond Carver earlier, you **referred to** the Beef Trust. Could you **tell us a little more** about that?
3. When you were **describing** the Swedish model, you **said that** without male demand there would be no female supply. I **wonder if** this is not somewhat utopian.
4. When you were **describing** Cholesky factorizations, you **mentioned that** total number of FLOPs decreases by a factor of approximately 4 in going down one tree level. Could you **explain** this in **some more detail**, or perhaps **give an example**?
5. When you were **discussing** juvenile delinquents, you **made the point that** some feel that too much affluence can lead to aimlessness and delinquency. Could you **be more specific** about that?

Exercise 1.5

1. about / on / concerning / regarding
2. exactly
3. back to
4. arrive
5. correctly / basically
6. fully
7. clear
8. on

Exercise 1.6

1. I'm afraid I don't quite follow.
2. Perhaps I didn't make myself clear.
3. Let me put it another way.
4. Where exactly do you stand on this issue?
5. Perhaps I could return to that point later on?
6. I wonder if I could comment on that last point.
7. I don't know that off the top of my head.
8. I don't think it's quite as simple as that.
9. I am not quite clear on what you mean.
10. I am sorry, but could you explain in a little more detail?

Exercise 2.1

1. It's perhaps not quite as bad as that ...
2. I don't think it's quite as simple as that
3. Not quite, not entirely, To a certain extent yes, but ..., yes, up to a point but, I agree in principle, but ...
4. would argue that ... / it seems to me ... / Personally, I'm convinced that ...
5. Could I just get back to the conclusion?

Exercise 2.2

1. I'm **afraid** I don't see the connection.
2. Can I get **back** to you on that?
3. Well, **as** I said earlier ...
4. To be honest, I think that raises a different **issue**
5. That's not something I've had time to **deal** with, but ...
6. Well, to be **honest**, I'm not really the right person to ask about that.
7. Sorry, could I **just** finish?
8. Perhaps I didn't make myself **clear**. What I was trying to say was ...
9. Anyway, I will **leave** it there for now.

Exercise 2.3

1. in mind
2. back to
3. at first glance
4. off the top
5. brought that up
6. getting at
7. on the whole
8. to the best of
9. depends on
10. wrap it up

2. Chairing a conference session

Exercise 1.1 53

1. Can everyone see **clearly**?
2. You're blocking the **view** this way.
3. There's a **remote** available if you would like to use one.
4. I will show you a **cue card** with a five-minute announcement.

1. Our **final** speaker today is …
2. She will be here **shortly**. Until that time we'd like to have a 10-15 minute **recess**.
3. Is that the right **pronunciation**?
4. Am I **pronouncing** this correctly?

1. Could you perhaps speak a little **louder**?
2. Could you speak **up** a little?
3. The screen's gone **blank**.

1. I'm afraid I really have to cut you **short** here.
2. we're **running** out of time.

1. I do not know who would like to **kick off**.
2. I am **sure** you will have many questions.
3. OK, we have **about** fifteen minutes for questions and discussion. Would **anyone / anybody** like to start?
4. We have **some** more time
5. We actually have **plenty** of time for discussion.

1. OK, there, 2nd row **at** the back.
2. Here **on** my left.
3. I think there are other people **that / who** have questions.
4. There're other people that had their hand up so let's go to **somebody/someone** else and then we can circle back to you when other people have had a **chance** to speak.
5. Sorry to **cut** you **short**, but I'm hoping to **move on** to the next part of the debate.
6. Okay, one last question before we **wrap** this **up**.
7. I think we have time for one last question before we **break** for lunch.

Exercise 2.1 58

1. He received his Ph.D …
2. Since then, he has taken …
3. He has published widely …
4. Last year he was elected …
5. he spent a year at Warwick.
6. These questions have become increasingly prominent …

Key to the Exercises

Exercise 2.2   59
1. This is the topic that she is working on
2. He is currently writing a thesis entitled ...
3. Her main interests lie in ...
4. More specifically, she is studying the effect of ...
5. I'm very pleased to present to you (or: introduce) Antonio X.

3. Tutoring students

Exercise 2.1   65
1. What **do / would you suggest?** (*what are you suggesting?* might sound hostile)
2. Is that what **you're saying?**
3. I **was thinking of possibly going into genetic research.**
4. What other courses **do / would you think I should take?**
5. I **was wondering what kind of classes I should be taking**

Part Three

1. Expanding vocabulary

Exercise 1.1

1. set us back – 2. embarked on / behind schedule – 3. set out – 4. back on track – 5. get off the ground – 6. start from scratch – 7. put on hold – 8. made considerable progress

Exercise 1.2

1. catch up on – 2. up to my eyes – 3. taken up – 4. got round to it – 5. pressed for time – 6. on a tight schedule – 7. overcommitted

Exercise 1.3

1. memory – 2. heart – 3. mind – 4. sieve – 5. tongue – 6. brains – 7. blank – 8. mind – 9. bell

Exercise 1.4

1. relevant – 2. comprehensive – 3. reasonable – 4. thought-provoking — 5. lively – 6. inspiring
1. blend – 2. covered – 3. understanding – 4. provoked – 5. eye-opener – 6. well-argued

Exercise 1.5

1. cracked – 2. desired – 3. par – 4. sighted – 5. effective – 6. obscure

Exercise 1.6

1. To make matters worse, ...
2. To put it mildly, ...
3. To cut a long story short, ...
4. To put it in a nutshell, ...
5. To start the ball rolling, ...
6. To put that another way, ...

Exercise 1.7

The missing word is *mind*

Exercise 1.8

1. point – 2. round – 3. wavelength – 4. lost – 5. across – 6. responsive

Exercise 1.9

1. details – 2. detail – 3. details – 4. details – 5. detail

Exercise 1.10

1. first come, first served – 2. take for granted – 3. easier said than done – 4. leaves a lot to be desired – 5. getting sidetracked – 6. that said

Exercise 1.11

1. to – 2. off – 3. on – 4. with – 5. as – 6. at – 7. to

Exercise 1.12

1. tackle a problem – 2. lose sight of – 3. paved the way – 4. carry a lot of weight – 5. jump to conclusions – 6. bridge the gap – 7. make sense – 8. overlook the fact – 9. drawing the wrong conclusion – 10. gaining ground

Exercise 1.13

1. a foregone conclusion
2. in due course
3. plain sailing
4. a much broader range
5. prove useful
6. sketchy
7. narrow in scope
8. a valid point
9. overwhelming evidence
10. consistent with

Exercise 1.14

1. narrow down – 2. pass round – 3. switch off – 4. plug in – 5. turned up – 6. boils down to – 7. ties in – 8. rule out – 9. weigh up the options – 10. get across – 11. comes down to

Exercise 1.15

1. pick up on
2. come back to that
3. at this stage
4. bring us up to date
5. the key to analysing such data
6. To my knowledge

Exercise 1.16

1. came up with
2. take on board
3. By and large
4. state of the field

Exercise 1.17

1. go hand in hand
2. tie in closely with
3. relate to each other
4. interrelated
5. strongly associated with
6. inextricably linked
7. intertwined
8. intimately connected
9. lumped together

2. Avoiding common errors

Exercise 1.1

- tell: tell someone something
- say: say something to someone // say that
- explain: explain something to someone // explain that
- discuss: discuss something

1. What I would like to do is present my research to you
2. Let me first explain what the research questions are
3. I'll tell you something about methodology first / I'll say something about methodology first
4. As I said earlier / As I told you earlier
5. I will make some remarks about >
6. I would just like to say that you can interrupt me >
7. We're discussing the causes now >

Exercise 1.2

1. contrary to … / in contrast
2. regarding the first aspect / with regard to the first aspect
3. concerns a subject
4. at least as far as the climate was concerned
5. a couple of criticisms
6. apart from these colonists / besides these colonists
7. at a very initial stage
8. You are mistaken if you think that …
9. Can you deduce the implications?
10. I'll briefly describe
11. economic problems
12. monitor / check up on
13. Finally, I would like …

Key to the Exercises

Exercise 1.3

1. react to that information
2. characteristics of
3. focus on
4. If the consumer is satisfied with
5. when you want to go to / attend a conference
6. should apply to
7. answers to
8. on some occasions

Exercise 1.4

1. when we look at ...
2. concerned with
3. come back to.
4. ask Ø the person if
5. at a disadvantage
6. keep in mind
7. in the long term
8. discuss Ø this

Exercise 1.5

1. a classic example
2. give criticism
3. briefly describe
4. interrupt / cut in
5. optional literature
6. evolved

Exercise 2.1

1. a **widely** accepted definition
2. a **typically** Belgian problem
3. **purely** technical matters
4. **well** established / not **surprising**
5. very **well** structured
6. very **briefly**
7. **easy** to follow
8. **voluntarily**
9. very **brief**
10. more **specifically**
11. **freely** downloadable
12. **automatically** generates
13. how **quickly** we can
14. is **typical** of
15. do this **unconsciously**

Exercise 2.2 86

1. Are you only looking at causes **then**?
2. A scriptfile **always** has the extension .exp.
3. I started my post-doctoral fellowship **this year**. (This year, I ... started)
4. I would insert an article **there**.
5. I **sometimes** had the impression that you were hesitating.
6. Most of the literature is in English **as well**.
7. You should focus on the immediate effects **more**.
8. You can see two reactions **here**.

1. (**Now**)You can (**now**) go to Toledo (**now**).
2. (**Now**) They (**now**) take a stricter approach (**now**).
3. (**Now**) This matrix (**now**) has two rows and four columns (**now**).

Now at the start of the sentence is very emphatic.

1. You can **already** conduct some analysis on a newspaper article.
2. Of course we've **already** omitted the details here.
3. The logo **already** exists in Spain
4. The word itself **already** says what its characteristics are.

1. We **also** do that quite often.
2. We **also** have to be aware that ...
3. In this way, you **also** obtain a chi-square value
4. In order to understand, you **also** have to look at ...

Exercise 2.3 86

1. in Ø both studies
2. She is **a** member of ....
3. In Ø Roman imperial times ...
4. This work is **a** classic.
5. It is **a** different subdivision.
6. It's Ø good advice
7. He's **a** philosopher.
8. ... revealed by Ø multivariate analysis.
9. discussions concerning **the** nature of Ø rationality.
10. a multiple-choice design with Ø most questions having four or five choices.

Exercise 2.4 87

1. When this country **becomes** a member, there *will be* ....
2. It *would have been* clearer if you **had used** more examples.
3. If supermarkets **offered** more ... , consumers *would* automatically *buy* more.
4. If I **had** to choose, I *would take* the second part.
5. If they *had been attacked*, they **would have reported** it.
6. The lecturer suggested I contact you to see if you **would schedule** an extra tutorial. (= polite request)

Exercise 2.5

1. I'm allowed to use this material **if** I acknowledge them in the Foreword.
2. **If** you were to believe that, you would be irrational.
3. I'll check up on this **when** I get back to the office.
4. Maybe you can finish that **when** class is over.
5. Well, I'd be really surprised **if** this really helped reduce crime rates.

Exercise 2.6

1. so **many** pieces
2. **little** evidence that
3. had **many** setbacks
4. a **number** of students
5. put as **many** new products on the market as possible
6. a **few** of these examples.
7. so that there are **many** more linkages
8. Most pay **little** attention
9. **much** time
10. a large **number** of problems

Exercise 2.7

1. a brand **that** is actually better than ...
2. schools **that** teach Cornish
3. a part **that** I'm currently working on
4. a student **who** ...
5. the people **that / who**
6. project **that / which**
7. ..., **which** was
8. islands, **which** are
9. the debate **that / which**
10. the man **who / that**

Exercise 2.8

1. have manifested **themselves**
2. the cells **themselves**
3. think for **himself**
4. switch **it** on
5. do this **ourselves**

Exercise 2.9

1. we need to take into account the buildings that **existed**.
2. I**'ve** only **been working** on this for 2 months
3. It **has existed** for two years
4. The study **deals** with ...

5. She **had** already **been** in Leuven for 2 before I arrived.
6. I**'ve been living** in Leuven for 3 years
7. Since then, she **has worked** in the History department.
8. This here **represents** an amount of biomass.
9. From here on, Chapter two **starts**.
10. I**'ve taught / been teaching** this course for 4 years.

Exercise 2.10   91
1. and the last reason why **I don't agree** with ...
2. They are **used to buying** books over the Internet.
3. customers that **have** already **switched**
4. What exactly **does** ... **mean?**
5. I don't mind **answering** these questions.
6. I agree with most things that **have** already **been said.**
7. I**'ll give** you 5 minutes for that.
8. Ok, I**'ll start** with a definition of the main concepts.

Exercise 2.11   92
1. *is it* only the specialists ...
2. *they / these are* efficient markets
3. *these are* the brands that ...
4. as you can see, *it was* ... / *these were* ...
5. but *these are* details
6. we call *these* ...
7. *these are* the types
8. *it is* the genes that

Exercise 2.12   92
1. some anomalies **exist / there are**, however, ...
2. and **it was said that** ...
3. **can anything** be done?
4. poverty and **its** effect on children
5. not **my PhD topic** / the **topic of my Ph.D.**
6. I conducted **a study** on
7. **some** information
8. not **all over** Belgium
9. people who are a **party member**
10. a colleague **of ours** said that ...
11. **What** is it called
12. We wanted **there to be** a distinction between ...
13. **Either** it is man-made, **or** it is ...
14. a model of **what** wires on a chip look like
15. (A number of) **Modern editions have been made**